AMERICAN
BOOK
OF THE
DEAD

OTHER BOOKS BY E.J. GOLD

Alchemical Sex
American Book of the Dead, Practitioner's Edition (2004)
Angels Healing Journey
The Book of Sacraments
Creation Story Verbatim
The Great Adventure
The Hidden Work
The Human Biological Machine
as a Transformational Apparatus
The Invocation of Presence (Private Publication)
The Joy of Sacrifice
Life in the Labyrinth
The Lost Works of E.J. Gold (Limited Edition)
Practical Work on Self
The Seven Bodies of Man
Tanks for the Memories (with Dr. John C. Lilly)
Visions in the Stone

On the occasion of the 30th anniversary of the **American Book of the Dead**, Gateways Books would like to acknowledge the special contributions made by the book's first trade publisher, Sebastian Orfali (1946-1997) of And/Or Press; the illustrators of the first two public editions, artists Lauren Elder and George Metzger; and all those individuals over the years who have contributed to support this profoundly beneficial publishing project, whether they contributed money, skilled labor, enthusiasm, dedication, or energy in any form. Thanks and blessings also to everyone over the years who has read the guiding instructions for any Voyager. We hope you will continue this practice and become one of the Labyrinth Readers of the *American Book of the Dead*.

E.J. GOLD, *DEATH COMES AS A LOVER*, CHARCOAL ON ARCHES PAPER, 1987.

AMERICAN
BOOK
OF THE
DEAD

WRITTEN AND ILLUSTRATED BY

E.J. GOLD

GATEWAYS/IDHHB, INC.
PUBLISHERS

Some material in this book has appeared in its present form
or in earlier textual versions in the following publications:

American Book of the Dead—First Edition, limited, © 1974
The American Book of the Dead—Revised Standard Practitioner's Edition, © 1975
American Book of the Dead—Trade Edition, And/Or Press, © 1975
American Book of the Dead—Standard Revised Edition, Doneve Designs, © 1978
New American Book of the Dead—Practitioner's Edition, © 1980
New American Book of the Dead—Trade Edition, © 1981
The Lazy Man's Guide to Death & Dying—Limited Edition, © 1983
The Lazy Man's Guide to Death & Dying—Trade Edition, © 1983, 1984
The Original American Book of the Dead, © 1987
The American Book of the Dead—Trade Edition, Harper San Francisco, © 1995
The Original American Book of the Dead, Revised Edition, © 1990, 1993, 1999

All Rights Reserved, Printed in the USA, Tenth Printing
Published by Gateways Books & Tapes
IDHHB, Inc., PO Box 370, Nevada City, CA 95959
(800) 869-0658 or (530) 477-8101, FAX: (530) 272-0184

Gold, E.J.
American book of the dead / written and illustrated by E.J.
Gold – Nevada City, CA : Gateways/IDHHB, c1987
xx, 196 p. : ill. ; 22 cm.
Cover title: The original American book of the dead
ISBN: 0-89556-051-8 (pbk.) : $15.95

1. Future life. 2. Death. 3. Reincarnation. I. Title II. Title: Original
American book of the dead.
BF1311.F8G64   1987   133.9—dc19   87-82942
                 AACR 2 MARC
Library of Congress

TABLE OF CONTENTS

E.J. GOLD, *THE REALIZATION*, CHARCOAL ON RIVES BFK, 1992.

Behold a child
Naked is he,
He comes not into the world
For he is not of woman born,
He is called Oldest.

Havama, Norse 9th Century Bardic Lay

It's when you first get up in the morning
And smell your own breath
And sit on the john to let out
The day's first blast
Of methane and sulphur dioxide
That it hits home the hardest . . .
The whole system
Operates on rot.

It isn't just the body,
That fabulous human machine,
That tip-to-toe mass of organic decay
in seething fury to survive,
One microorganism over another,
Fighting like fury to stay on top,
Dominating the dung heap for a single moment
And succumbing the next,
That walking, talking
Semiplastic garbage bag
With the slim semblance
Of Intelligence and Purpose.

And here you are
Sitting smack dab in the middle of it all,
Right in the center of the swamp,
A king or queen riding the wild horse of rot,
And here's another box of cereal about to
Become one with the human host,
Another few hours of fodder
For the great compost heap,
Fueling it for the day ahead.
Steeling itself for meaningful deeds,
Girding its loins for the far-reaching,
Earth-shaking events,
The sky-piercing thoughts,
All-embracing transdimensional visions,
The subtle shadings of emotional delights,
Lover and beloved
Gazing with rapturous lustful wonder
A swooning, sweeping, swaying dance of love,
An interlude of romance,
A moment's brush with beauty,
Another afternoon of love,
Another sexy bag of rot.

20th Century North American Bardic Lay

EDITOR'S FOREWORD

All of us at Gateways Books & Tapes are proud to publish this 30th anniversary edition of E.J. Gold's *American Book of the Dead*. This was the first book by the author to achieve national distribution and international prominence. It was the first book from Gateways (then IDHHB Publishing, in 1974) to be printed by another trade publisher. By the time it was issued as a reprint in 1995 by Harper & Row, it had achieved the status of a "consciousness classic." We would like to thank Mr. Gold for his ongoing efforts on behalf of all Beings everywhere. After thirty years of keeping his influential and beneficial book continuously in print, we anticipate continuing its run through our own era and beyond for the children of the twenty-first century.

I'll repeat here what I wrote for the 1993 Gateways edition: a Book of the Dead is not strictly a book for the dead but a book for all labyrinth voyagers, all those who wake up dead, deep in one kind of sleep or another. We are all voyagers. In one part of the voyage we are attached to a biological machine. In another part of the voyage, we find ourselves without a biological machine to refer to. But it is all the same labyrinth, and all the same voyage. And that is why a book of the dead is not only for the organically dead but for all voyagers—no matter what dimensional level of the labyrinth they may be exploring at the moment. If we are able to make this voyager's book our own, we may be able to bring its transdimensional technology into the world beyond organic life, and to be of service to other voyagers as well as ourselves.

Iven Lourie
Grass Valley, 2005

PREFACE

In Shambhala Bookstore in Berkeley, where I live—at the center of that cultural cyclone that has variously manifested as a psychedelic revolution, civil rights movement, the Human Potential Movement, and, generally speaking, that New Age that has reached most of our problematic world—there is, in addition to sections on Taoism, Hinduism, Buddhism, Sufism, Esoteric Christianity, and "Fourth Way" books, and so on, a section entitled "Individual Teachers." There, along with books by Krishnamurti, Rajneesh, and others, one has seen over the last decade or so a number of books by E.J. Gold.

I am not sure that it is possible to define what kind of a teacher Mr. Gold is without saying some interesting things in the process. So I have welcomed the opportunity to write this preface. Yet I welcome it especially in view of the high regard and admiration that I have had occasion to develop toward Mr. Gold through my years of acquaintance with his many activities.

I hesitated between writing "his activity" or using the plural (as I finally did)—for I see him as always and above all a teacher, but lately his paintings have attracted public attention, and at other times he has been a writer, a musician, a puppet master, a fasting fakir on public display, and an art dealer.

And a jester.

In an editorial of *Saturday Evening Wings Magazine* (circa 1975) he rightfully called himself "the Gadfly of the Human Potential Movement."

E.J.—as Mr. Gold is called by his intimates—has only been available to the limited number of students in a "low profile" spiritual community that more appears to be a series of business ventures than a monastery. Indeed, it is not open to seekers who are looking for themselves, but only to people who are ready to serve.

Just as the apprentices to Rembrandt or Verrochio learned by helping their masters, there are some who helping E.J. do "his" work, find at the same time meaningful lives and the stimulus of his influence.

When I met Mr. Gold he was called "Beast" and seemed a reincarnation of Gurdjieff's spirit. In the course of the years following, he not only taught awareness development through ordinary work and plain suffering, as Gurdjieff did, but was both sharp and tough in the confrontation of people's egos.

By the time he became "E.J." he had already started the writing of what was eventually published as *The Gabriel Papers* (currently titled *Creation Story Verbatim*). Since I read *The Tales of Beelzebub to His Grandson*, in my late adolescence, I had felt the imprint of Gurdjieff's mind on my own as forcefully as if he had been a grandfather—yet never before reading Gold's imitation had I been so conscious of Gurdjieff's strategy of holding the carrot before the reader's eyes, from page to page and chapter to chapter, forever promising the delivery of some esoteric secret and acting on his mind along the way in a completely different manner than expected, and through seemingly irrelevant material.

It is relevant to speak here about this particular book of E.J.'s because it might be said that the *American Book of the Dead* (or "ABD") is to The *Tibetan Book of the Dead* what *Creation Story Verbatim* is to Gurdjieff's esoteric narrative: a take-off and a book full of humor—yet also a book full of wisdom, and one through which some teachings in the original become more explicit or accessible to the many.

I had been personally exposed to a trickster-guru in the person of Ichazo—also a "Fourth Way" teacher—who similarly employed the carrot (along with the whip) in his approach—but never have I come across a trickster like Mr. Gold. Yet the unique thing about Mr. Gold is that he is a trickster and at the same time a very plain person who, unlike the stage-magician, doesn't mind giving away his tricks. To give an example, *Secret Talks by Mr. G.* has been thought by many to contain talks by Gurdjieff, yet those who know that Mr. G. stands for Mr. Gold, appreciate his imitation: his artistry at the same time mocks the orthodox Gurdjieff imitators and manages to say important things along the way.

In both cases I see an expression of E.J.'s unique way of presenting profound truth in vulgar garb. Dr. Charles Muses, mathematician and former editor of *The Journal for Altered States of Consciousness*, once remarked that Gold's comic book of *The Creation Story Verbatim* was not aesthetic, and then I became aware of the issue for the first time: not only is his presentation of esoteric material typically not aesthetic, but also he seems to purposely exaggerate the vulgar—as if to leave behind the all-too-academic, well-mannered or excessively aesthetic-minded reader. It is as if he wanted to create a barrier through such vulgar form—a barrier only negotiable to those who can receive a spiritual message without the need of "spiritual" language.

The ABD might be called the ABC of the bardos in comic-strip style.

By ABD I mean a series of editions and variations about the theme of the intermediate state and preparation for it.

The book purports to be advice on how to stay imperturbable in the midst of life and, more, to work toward higher consciousness under the stimulus of adverse conditions. Yet in the same way as Leary along with Alpert (now Ram Dass) and Metzner proposed that reading from *The Tibetan Book of the Dead* could serve as a vehicle for the navigation of psychedelic space, I know of those who have similarly resorted to the ABD.

Whatever the good that the ABD may bring in terms of awareness in daily life in preparation for an afterlife or as a stimulus for visionary experience, I think that it undeniably recommends itself to us as a structured contemplative journey (profound notwithstanding its Disney style)—a journey in which it becomes a magic carpet for us in the same measure in which we let ourselves yield to its promptings.

It only remains for me to wish buyers and borrowers of the book an entranced reading.

Claudio Naranjo
Santa Gadea del Cid (Spain), August 30, 1994

E.J. GOLD, *ME AND MY SHADOW,* CHARCOAL ON ARCHES PAPER, 1987.

AUTHOR'S PREFACE

"Hello—I've come to say I cannot stay, I must be going . . . I'll stay the weekend through, I'll stay a week or two but I am telling you . . . I must be going."

—**Groucho Marx,** from the movie *Animal Crackers*

This is really the book I didn't want to write. They all say that—but I really mean it. If there had been anything I could have done to avoid it, I would have.

You know, for years I really believed everyone knew all about this stuff, and that they were joking when they claimed no knowledge. It wasn't until 1974—local time calculation based on earth's (a mythological planet resembling a living being in space) revolutions around an equally mythological sun—that I discovered that this teaching had been neglected completely, and then finally lost, in the Western world.

Of course there are a lot of folks around now to help out with it. The Tibetans arrived here in large numbers, settling mostly in Berkeley, California, because it's the closest in climate and landscape to their native country.

They have the knowledge, but they don't have the language skills and cultural psychological background to communicate that knowledge to donkeys—I mean, Americans.

Since the original publication of this manuscript, the teaching has arrived in the form of many refugees and visitors from the far and near east. And like all things, there's a reason for that, too.

Just as the lobes of the human brain periodically transfer activity from one to the other, left to right and right to left, so does the teaching, the dharma, transfer from one hemisphere of the world to the other.

Every six or seven hundred years, like clockwork, the dharma—the spirit of the living earth—traverses West to East or East to West. Thus the male and female principles, teachers of the age, appear from time to time. In the East, and we're not talking about

Boston, Massachusetts, the tenth avatar has already come and gone. And so came the end for the dharma in the East.

Now for the next six hundred years there will appear in the West, tulkus, and avatars, and holy ones, and appearances of the Son and of the Mother endlessly *nudging* human primates to dig themselves out of sleep, and for some—a very few—there will be an awakening, and for the rest, a religion and maybe even several religions.

Meanwhile in the East, humanity will sleep awhile, wrapped in the thin comfort of high technology; their waking day is finished for the moment. But never fear; the time will come again when it is their turn to hold the dharma, their turn to hold the spirit within the world, their turn to labor in the world of being, and your turn to grab some shut-eye.

Ten avatars will come; each will take a rightful turn in the effort to maintain the waking state, thus earning a period—always far too short—of rest and relaxation.

The time of each avatar is set by law, and thus their dawning and setting is determined. Now the time of the first avatar, Ueuecoyotl, has come. And the first tulkus are already here. We will be with you for the next six hundred years and then we will leave. Our task will have been completed.

So this book is the result of the usual combination of teaching, being taught, and experience with these states and their consequences. Actually there are quite a few individuals around who do know about these things, as you'll soon discover if you begin to fool around and actually experiment with these states and ideas.

It just may occur that, as you learn to handle death and rebirth, you might learn to handle life in the process. This is unavoidable, and if by chance you do happen to handle life better because of it, don't despair; you'll never get out of it alive.

These readings for the voyager are the direct teachings of the guides—perhaps you think of them as teachers, sufis, arhats, bodhisattvas—and the instructions have been rendered into modern American usage.

If you have any trouble following and applying these instructions, you might want to inquire through the publisher about further study material which expands the subject and treats it more in depth and detail.

Now, you should remember the state that a voyager in the labyrinth gets into while still attached to a biological machine as well as between lives in the non-biological macrodimensions; it's a state of extreme lucidity, so don't worry if you have trouble understanding the meaning of the text, because the voyager in the labyrinth—with that all-embracing clarity of vision and understanding—won't have that problem. It's only in the form of human primates living in the lower dimensions that we need footnotes.

And by the way, if you're wondering about the source of this book, it comes directly from the source of all books. In the labyrinth, you'll notice—if you notice anything at all—that all books are the same book, and that they all say the same thing. Don't look around for someone else to hang it on . . . You are the source.

AMERICAN
BOOK
OF THE
DEAD

E.J. Gold, *Hybrid Satyr*, Charcoal on Arches paper, 1987.

NOTES ON THE LABYRINTH

So long as we seem to be *somewhere*, we can be sure that we are voyagers and that we are in the labyrinth—whether we perceive ourselves as possessing a biological machine or not.

The experience between death and rebirth carries with it an unforgettable experience of forgetfulness and an ego-shattering disintegration which for the inexperienced voyager can be very unsettling, destroying any conscious connection from one lifetime to another.

The attention of the voyager is designed to carry over and through many different bodies in many different times and conditions, but if the attention is shattered by the sudden disruption of macrodimensional transitions, it can only be attributed to the fact that the voyager didn't get familiarized with labyrinthine voyaging when the opportunity presented itself—which is now.

Of course, all this labyrinth voyaging is simply "bait" to get you to liberate yourself through this or any other process that develops.

Many cultures—except, of course, the post-Native-American culture—have always been well-informed about the between-lives state, and many voyagers have easily achieved liberation by passing through the terminal transition with an awakened attention. But this can only be achieved *during the lifetime*.

If it's so easy—you may well ask—why doesn't everybody do it? Well, like most things, doing it requires actually doing it, and for most of us, it's like going to the dentist; we don't want to go until the pain becomes unbearable, and in the case of labyrinth voyaging, by the time the pain becomes unbearable, it's too late to do anything but grit your non-phenomenal teeth and bear it until it's all over and you're spit out of the macrodimensions and slammed into yet another biological body.

But once you learn to voyage, it's like falling off a bicycle; once you've learned how, you never forget how, and even years and years later, you can get on a bike and fall right off as if it were only yesterday.

As one voyages through the labyrinth in the section between lives in a biological machine or other, one must have help. One must remain awake and alert, the full attention centered and self-sufficient.

The reader remains constant to this aim, guiding the voyager through the shocking ambushes of sudden macrodimensional transitions, so that the voyager may attain the highest possible state. Here, in this text, is the method for achieving an expanded lifespan not for the purpose of amusing oneself with "immortality"—which human beings already have, in the worst possible way, being immortal in the sense of permanent existence within a time-frame in the time-space discontinuum of creation—but solely for the purpose of perfection of the self, to help in the Great Work, the aim of which is the liberation and awakening of something much higher than oneself.

One of the common responses to this teaching is to ask why do we worry about something that isn't right here, right now? First of all, it is imperative to understand that we don't even have a word in the language to describe the state between death and birth, and we don't have a word for the state itself, either. That means that although we do have a word for the other parts of reality in existence, that is birth, life and death, one of the four parts of reality is occluded or ignored in the common consciousness of the Westerner.

The fact that this necessary part of life has been totally occluded in our western awareness is related to the fact that life itself has been misunderstood because if one realized that we do in fact live in a multidimensional labyrinth, one would also realize that the labyrinth extends in all directions, not just those four minor dimensions which we speciously call space and time—it doesn't suddenly pop up out of nowhere just so one can get lost a few times and turn around in circles. We are always in the labyrinth, and that is why we need either a book of the dead as a guide or a living guide as a guide. The book has its drawbacks and disadvantages, but it is admittedly far less expensive in any ordinary sense of the word than the ambulatory alternative.

E.J. Gold, *Snowden is Odin*, Charcoal on Arches paper, 1987.

HOW TO USE THIS BOOK

Excerpted from
The Professional Labyrinth Reader's Handbook

Just as a midwife assists birth, the reader of the *American Book of the Dead* assists voyagers who have passed into the macrodimensions to attain liberation or to achieve a conscious and deliberate rebirth on re-entry into the human dimension in which the voyager may select a living creature with which to associate; such symbiotic association is commonly called, from the organic view, a *lifetime*.

The reader gives this guidance through the correct application of the instructions for passage through a period of severe stress, as is the condition during the voyage in the labyrinth between death and rebirth.

Instructions are delivered to the voyager through readings, the lighting, atmospherics (augmented by incenses) and music often supplying the mood, acting as a sort of emotional "carrier-wave" modulated by the thought patterns and imposed images

suggested by the text. Readings can either be given in the presence
of the human biological machine or through an article formerly
possessed by the voyager or through a photograph of the voyager's
biological machine.

If a photograph is used as a contact element, it should be
transported to the reading chamber in a light-proof container;
cardboard wrapped with aluminum foil is recommended.

The package containing the photograph should be opened by
the reader only in the space in which the reading is to be performed.

The basic idea of using an article—such as a photograph—
and a familiar sound—such as the name, with which the voyager
will automatically identify, and reading in the presence of the biological machine, is to establish a communication bonding that will
tend not to break during the disorientation in the between-lives
state in the labyrinth.

The optimum method of bonding reader and voyager is to
establish a good communication and friendship before the voyager
enters the labyrinth, primarily through frequent practice readings.
However, where there was no previous contact, it is possible to
establish a good bond by using the name, place and time of entry
into the between-lives state, such as the hospital, home or scene of
accident, any location which would help the voyager fix the attention on the reading, age at time of terminus (physical death) and a
good physical description of the individual; then through visualizing the voyager mentally, reading to that visualized form.

The essential point is to establish contact, and the best contact is established on mental and emotional levels of visualization.

While material objects may be used to make initial contact,
the readings and instructions are actually directed toward the voyager in spiritual form, not toward the human biological machine or
material objects. Once contact has been definitely established, the
reader is able to deliver labyrinth-guiding instructions with certainty. Sudden loss of contact, which can be tangibly felt by the
reader, usually means that the individual has taken rebirth.

How can one be certain that contact has been established? Definite sensations and perception changes are associated with contact.

To begin with, one understands every word of the instructions when one reads them. If words seem slurred or unintelligible to us, we're probably not in contact and the instruction is not being received. The reason one understands the instructions when contact is good is that the bond which has been established confers the clarity of understanding from the voyager to the reader.

Some of the sensations indicating that good contact has been established are:

• A tingling at the back of the neck.

• A slight feeling of imbalance, as if the room tilted, and a sensation of disorientation, as if one really didn't have all that vertigo.

• Hearing and visual perception greatly heightened. Sometimes there is an uncanny quiet during the readings, as if everything outside had suddenly come to a complete halt while labyrinth instructions are delivered.

• Some readers have reported that they got "a funny feeling in the gut," or "the top of my head felt as if it opened up and I could hear things for miles and see through the walls."

Each of these are simply indicators that tell us that we are in strong communication with the voyager.

Our own perceptions, sensations and feelings may be radically different from the examples given above, but one thing is certain—when we do definitely establish contact with someone in the between-lives state, we'll feel sensations and perceptual changes as a result.

If we establish contact with someone in the between-lives state, our biological machine and being-attention will tend to vibrate sympathetically. This phenomenon is called *resonance*.

This is the same phenomenon that occurs when one strikes a C-tuned tuning fork and holds it next to another C-tuned fork. The second tuning fork, even though unstruck, will begin to vibrate along with the first one. Sound can create sympathetic motion, and thus can be used, like photon-driven solar sails, to move an individual through the labyrinth. As one learns from using the teaching and reading it aloud, sound has tremendous power—it can heal, liberate, awaken and even amuse.

When reader and voyager are vibrating in sympathetic resonance, it seems as if we are reading to ourselves—*but for the benefit of another*, and so a strong sonic and emotional reverberation results.

The reader can help to improve the chances that the individual in the labyrinth does not have anything drawing him or her back. By arranging the events surrounding *Terminus*—the voyager's exit from the human dimension occasionally through intentional embarkation, perhaps an artificially induced out-of-the-body excursion or macrodimensional expansion, more often through the process of biological death—the reader can help cut the bonds of attachment for the voyager.

The more the family is allowed to participate, the less likely they will be to fall into sadness and grief, simply because the more they participate in the guiding process, the more they will understand death and dying as a means of freeing oneself for the ultimate adventure.

Under ordinary conditions the voyager will succumb to the force of unconsciousness from the moment of terminus and remain in a sleep state throughout the labyrinth voyage unless he or she has been specially prepared during life through visualization, emotional reinforcement—in the realm of transcendent moods—and frequent reading practice, lying prone and being read to, and reading to others.

One's basic aim in this respect is to reach the voyager before terminus and drill the instructions until they become drenched in habit, literally second-nature. Intentionally acquired macrodimensional habits can greatly enable the voyager to remain awake through ordinarily overwhelming events in the labyrinth, and when rebirth becomes inevitable, the reader can help by indicating specific bodies, times and spaces in which the voyager may choose to be reborn—a lifetime in which the voyager may be able to accomplish the next lifetime's purpose in the voyager's evolutionary spiral.

It can be said that the reader is responsible for selecting options for a labyrinth voyager who has no decision-making mental equipment. Of course, this is not necessary for those who have made efforts to apply the teaching in life by working on themselves, developing a resistance to stress and a high degree of being-attention. They should have learned how to make good decisions *with the essential self*, without the need for rational linear brain-reasoning. Such individuals no longer need a mind with which to think. This condition of essential self was called in Zen the attainment of "*no mind*," which means "no mind, but plenty of attention, and interest without hunger and desire."

The voyager need not wonder whether or not this data will be there when it is needed, because it will be. Even for those who have practiced the teaching in life, through constant intentional stress, visualization and psycho-emotional reinforcement, readings are performed as a back-up just in case something should go wrong . . . go wrong . . . go wrong . . . .

It should be a relief to know that no matter what happens, there is a reader out there somewhere who has the sensitivity and integrity to deliver labyrinth instructions at the precise point at which they are needed and not a moment before, and that no matter how far from the human dimension we may wander, help is always available at extreme need, the operant words being "need" and "extreme."

As we learn more about the states between death and rebirth, we learn more about ourselves as immortal beings, and tend to regard death and dying not as evil or fearsome, but as just another rather uncomfortable and often inconvenient part of the voyage in and through the space-time discontinuum.

The labyrinth, too, loses its gargantuan proportions and the macrodimensions take on another, more real, perspective, or rather a complete lack of perspective, as the reality-holography which is, the universe flattens and softens into a sphere of plastic perceptions. Rebirth no longer is a bogeyman, and the material universe is less of a nightmare or no greater a nightmare than it has been all along.

After the doctors and nurses have given up trying to keep the body alive and the voyager trapped in the neural circuitry, and they have gone away, we'll be the only ones around with any idea of what to do next.

A doctor works to prevent death, but a reader does not try to prevent dying and death. Why, that's the first real opportunity for the voyager to get free of the biological machine and the incessant chatter of its restless little mind since the last time the voyager was in the between-lives section of the labyrinth!

The place of a reader during the period of macrodimensional voyaging is a position of primary importance, prominence and trust. It is occupied with dignity and integrity.

Above all, a reader must care—really care—what happens to another voyager. At the same time one cannot become identified with another voyager; the reader walks the fine line between total empathy and total non-attachment.

It is especially important that the reader be able to read aloud clearly and distinctly in order to provide the instruction necessary for the labyrinth voyager to be able to receive it and use it.

Here are the simple but essential skills we need to develop for reading:

1. *Read slowly and distinctly.* Many readers sound at first as if they're trying to win a race. You'll find that if you slow down even below the limit of slow speech tolerable for you, it will almost be too fast for a labyrinth instruction reading, unless you're

a professional actor or actress, in which case, just read normally, emote as necessary and never let them see you sweat.

2. *Read the instructions as if you had just thought of them.* If you find a word that isn't your own—that is, you don't know what it means—get it defined before going any further. *Don't, under any circumstances, substitute your own words for the words of the text when doing a reading.* Just find out what the words in the text mean. Use a dictionary if necessary. If you must ad-lib, do it on your own time.

3. *Read each passage as if for the first time.* Get the feeling of freshness about each idea as you read it; feel the newness of each instruction as you encounter it.

4. *Don't just read an instruction—deliver it!* Reading instructions means that there's no one at the other end. Delivering instructions means that there is someone there who is receiving them. The surest way to deliver an instruction is to know there is someone on the other end of your communication line.

5. *Read every instruction as if it is important for it to get through.* Think of the voyager as someone who will sink unless you get through with these instructions. Get the idea of being a flight controller giving emergency flight instructions to a stewardess on a commercial jetliner on which the pilot and copilot are knocked out. Hey! What a great idea for a film plot!

6. *Read with purpose and certainty.* The only way to do this really effectively is to feel it. And the only way to really feel it is to know that the teaching is a working system. The only way to know that is to experience it. *So make sure you get the experience of it.*

7. *Read what is actually there, not something you substituted.* Anyone who feels and understands the urgency and importance of getting clear and precise instructions to a labyrinth voyager will be careful enough to read the actual text. If you drift off, you may substitute other words for the words that are really in the book. *Make sure you give correct data, and the best way to do this is by training your attention not to wander.*

When reading to the voyager don't hurry; *interlocking resonance* ensures that you will be delivering the exact instruction at the exact moment that it is necessary. Interlocking resonance causes your instruction to coincide precisely with the exact stress point at which it applies.

An instruction contains as an integral part of its text the address-code encryption which directs its guiding force to that specific point of stress in the labyrinth to which it applies. In the macrodimensions, time is not a measure of events, but a function of space. A sequence of events occurs in its totality; the voyager moves through this frozen sequence as an actor might move across a stage. All moments are equally accessible, all space within easy reach. It is possible to do all the readings for a labyrinth voyager in one single day; even so, the subjective time-flow in the human dimension may appear to correspond to the voyage in periods of days, months and sometimes years.

Each reading in the text printed in boldface (dark type) is the exact address of each stress point in the labyrinth sequence. Delivering a precise reading for each instruction assures that the instruction will get to the point at which it is needed. Strike a bell before the boldface reading and again after the boldface reading, clearly parenthesizing the reading with sound for the voyager.

In the First Stage readings, a bell-strike is appropriate before and after each numbered reading. During the Second and Third Stage readings, use the bell-strike to begin and end the daily reading for that chamber. If you choose to read through the entire text for a voyager—which certainly cannot hurt and may be to the voyager's benefit—you should use the bell-strike before and after each **boldface (dark type)** reading to distinguish it as a stress point instruction, parenthesized by sound from the ordinary text.

You can mis-time the reading by an hour or more and still be sure that the reading will get to the point at which the being needs to apply it, but that's no reason to become careless, just because you know that there is a large tolerance in the timing of the readings. Specific times for readings are recommended; six a.m. and six p.m., because energy levels of the earth are affected by temperature and atmospherics, and under these early morning and early evening conditions, ambient atmospheric plasma and other electromagnetic phenomena are at an optimum for macrodimensional contact.

If you read at haphazard times, you will not get the energy to perform your task nearly as well as if you make it a daily habit— and it's another good method of reinforcement to make readings part of your daily life. You can do several readings for several voyagers in series by using the name and photograph to address each voyager, following this with the appropriate text. Some renunciants do this all day long, for as many as several hundred voyagers.

Get into the habit of doing the readings every morning and every evening at exactly the same time; say, six o'clock in the morning, and six in the evening. Then after a week of doing this, *don't do it one evening*. Notice a definite feeling of unused energy? *That's* why we do readings at the same time each day.

You will find that by doing these exercises you will begin to feel very good about reading aloud to anyone or even reading aloud to yourself. Think about it for a moment—when you are alone reading a book, are you actually *reading to no one?* Of course not. Yet many people will say that reading alone is reading to no one! That's like the old joke, "What does he do when he's alone?" "I don't know...I've never been with him when he's alone."

Constant practice and good discipline at maintaining your exercises will develop into a clear understanding of what you are doing as a reader. Good discipline in maintaining your exercises on a high level of energy input is the only way to achieve this. Only by putting the teaching into action will you really learn what this is all about! As you might have noticed, just *reading* about doing has no learning effect.

As you continue applying the teaching in action, you will inevitably become more and more aware of subtleties—and the terminology and structure of the teaching will begin to make practical sense. As this occurs, you will be able to see more and more ways in which you can apply the teaching in your everyday life to make you more able to handle your existence, to help others handle theirs, and ways to use these ideas in a whole body-mind-emotions spiritual healing technique, along with many other applications, not covered in this present volume, which are now available in home-study courses on videotape and in work-manuals.

During the first few readings, you may notice that you tend to lapse occasionally into inattention. You might want to be there for the reading, but your attention wanders before you can do anything about it. It may even be a minute or two before you notice that you seem to have unaccountably drifted off and that the words are coming out of your mouth, but that they've all become gabble and gibberish, like hearing someone in a dream, and you come out of it with a start, realizing that you aren't following the meaning of the text.

This has probably happened to you if you drive a car—you suddenly realize that you haven't been paying attention to anything for several minutes. Some people can drive for several hours without being really aware of what they've been doing. Everything just goes on "automatic pilot." In delivering labyrinth instructions, your attention must be focused directly and firmly on every single word that goes across, paying particular heed to the danger signal that contact is momentarily broken—a word, phrase, or visualization that you don't understand. Eventually, you will develop the ability to be there with *full attention* for every word, every phrase, every single instruction.

The specific remedy for wandering attention is to read *as if someone's life depended on it.* You can get the idea that the voyager is in danger unless you get the necessary instruction across. Sometimes a feeling of danger succeeds where the best mental intention fails. You can't maintain constant being-attention because the emotions of the biological machine will pull the being-attention into sleep. The trick is to arouse the emotions along with the being-attention. There are some easy ways to accomplish this.

I hesitate to bring this up only because it is another of those things that can't be handled in a book. It needs a coach and a supervised situation to give this kind of instruction. You should know that it is available, but only in a workshop situation.

Several remedies you could use without having to go through a special course to learn to arouse and maintain the emotional and physical attentions are available right now:

1. *Read as if you're reading the material for the first time.*

2. *Deliver the labyrinth instructions as if something terrible will happen if it doesn't get through.*

3. *Read as if the individual you're reading to will someday be reading for you while you are in the labyrinth, and will remember with joy . . . or bitterness . . . the job you did for them.*

Something else may suddenly occur to you as you're reading, so it might be well to mention it; you could well be projecting the scenario that you are not now in the between-lives state; that you are reading for someone else, a voyager in the macrodimensions, but you suddenly come to realize that it really is *you who is in the between-lives state!* We are very capable of creating for ourselves a protective mechanism, a semblance of ordinary, familiar reality to disguise what's really happening. *Now you have a good reason to read with attention, as if someone's very being depended on it. It might be your own.*

LABYRINTH READING SCHEDULE
Begin each reading with the Obligatory Reader's Invocation

DAY IN CYCLE	MACRODIMENSIONAL COORDINATES	READING
Day of Moment of Death	The Symptoms	Reading #1
	Entering Transition	Reading #2
	Address to the Voyager	Reading #3
	Confronting the Clear Light	Reading #4
	Secondary Clear Light	Reading #5
Day following Terminus	Confronting the Clear Light	Reading #4
3rd Day	Confronting the Clear Light	Reading #4
4th Day	Second Stage/First Apparition Manifestation of the Friendly Guides	Introduction / 4th Chamber
5th Day		5th Chamber
6th Day		6th Chamber
7th Day		7th Chamber
8th Day		8th Chamber
9th Day		9th Chamber
10th Day		10th Chamber
11th Day	Second Stage / Second Apparition Manifestation of the Unresponsive Guides	Introduction / 11th Chamber
12th Day		12th Chamber
13th Day		13th Chamber
14th Day		14th Chamber
15th Day		15th Chamber
16th Day		16th Chamber
17th Day		17th Chamber
18th Day	Third Stage / Reformation of Consciousness	Introduction / 18th Chamber
19th Day through 49th Day		19th Chamber through 49th Chamber

E.J. Gold, *Macrodimensional Lovers*, Charcoal on Arches Paper, 1987.

INTRODUCTION TO THE MACRODIMENSIONS OF THE LABYRINTH

The sheer ordinariness of an unprepared experience of the macrodimensional domains of the labyrinth deceives us into complacent acceptance of events; the unsuspecting voyager is unaware of any transition, and so the Tibetans, Navajo, Micronesians, Benin, and other cultural primitives—but macrodimensional sophisticates—have trained themselves through visualization to view all dimensions of the labyrinth, including the human dimension, in a supernormal way.

Without continuous well-reinforced visualization training, the labyrinthine macrodimensions tend to masquerade as ordinary life. Guides appear but we explain them to ourselves as simple changes of light playing tricks on the vision; the sweeping tonal harmonics of macrodimensional sounds we translate to common understandable phenomena—horns of passing traffic, airplanes, music—orchestral, choral, heavily metallic.

The mind transforms labyrinth phenomena into ordinary phenomena of the present consciousness. Remember that the nature of the phenomenal world—the lower dimensions—is phenomena. All the phenomena of the "organic" world—the human dimension—as well as the labyrinth with its macrodimensions are *controlled by the being-attention*, because higher mind controls itself—unlike lower mind which is controlled by the environment. But unfortunately, the awareness of an individual generally doesn't include awareness of, or control over, the mind.

What is called the "mind" in ordinary inter-cultural translations of higher ideas is simply the result of the activities of the primary attention of the being, the cosmic nature of which is voidness, which is called in this treatise the essential self—that which is one's own—the deepest self existing only temporarily dependently upon the biological self.

One of the primary problems with an untrained individual who has not inculcated within himself firsthand knowledge of the subtle feelings and sensations of the macrodimensional domains of the labyrinth, which during the lifetime are hidden under the dominant organic feelings, perceptions and sensations of organic life, is to actually notice the unusual non-organic nature of the macrodimensional environment without dropping into blackout, waking up only after it's all over.

A normal human primate, given the usual education and routinized life-experience, just doesn't have the slightest idea of what's going on—where he is, what's happening around him, his feelings and sensing, his sensations, the events proceeding all around him— not even one millionth of it. We can't expect to notice that anything is different in the macrodimensions of the labyrinth when the only difference is the *quality* of the experience and not the *imagery*.

That's why we need to train ourselves to feel, sense and be aware of ourselves and our environment: not to enhance our sex lives or personality, but to be sensitive to change on a much deeper level than the organic mind and its primate-level senses and values. It's also a good idea to establish a new imagery for our voyage in the labyrinth. We can't depend on a sudden increase in our sensitivity to small and subtle series of changes in the environment; it probably won't happen.

It isn't necessary to understand the readings. If understanding comes, that's fine, but the reading will reach the part of the person that's actually going into the macrodimensional domains of the labyrinth and in that state understanding comes naturally. Read this at every opportunity; and where it's disallowed or outlawed as "religious trash" by fanatics of primate and other forms of organic existence who would like to martyr every being and thus trap all beings in the organic human sector—then learn this method by heart and pass it on verbatim on an oral initiatory basis.

Cultivation of the fine art of dying requires great inner discipline, and for a population that doesn't even know about the macrodimensions, it's almost impossible to introduce. In a culture which has a taboo against knowing about death even on an ordinary organic level, it's going to take some doing!

Something very little known in the East and definitely unknown in the West is that the voyage in the labyrinth continues all the time; the labyrinth underlies the organic world; the vibrations of the macrodimensions of the labyrinth are dominated by the organic vibrations which are heavier and easier to sense through biological machine and human awareness than the direct but subtle perceptions of the dimensional domains.

Another fact: you can enter and leave the macrodimensions of the labyrinth *at any time* for periods of seconds, minutes, hours or years, up to eternities, and experience rebirth *not necessarily in an infant biological machine*. You can be reborn at any time and into *any* size, shape and age biological machine. Your subjective experience, unless you have had training in feeling and sensing, is as if nothing unusual had happened. All the experiences in the macrodimensional domains of the labyrinth tend to go unnoticed, and you may take subtle rebirth without knowledge or control. However, once in a biological machine, you insist that those are *your* memories and *your* interests and that you have *always* had *that biological machine*. After all, if you had been in the macrodimensional domains of the labyrinth and then been reborn into the present dimension, you'd know it—wouldn't you?

The ordinary individual changes habitation in each of the Six Lower Tertiary Dimensions without realizing it, anywhere from four to five times to hundreds of times *every few days*! But try explaining that to someone who couldn't tell you what's been going on for the last minute and a half.

Warning: Don't reach out trying to help those who don't want help. Help by quietly reading the labyrinth instructions out of earshot and out of sight. If they catch you helping them, they'll tar and feather you and run you out of town on a rail—that's a wooden post used for rural fencing, not the steel kind used for locomotives; just a human way of saying "Thanks!"

If you haven't had any training in the feeling and sensing exercises and you are in doubt about whether you're in the macrodimensions of the labyrinth or not, here are some suspicious places to look. The chances are very good that you are in the macrodimensional domains of the labyrinth if you suddenly, without segue, find yourself:

In a bus or train or plane or any other form of public "transportation."

Compulsively walking from room to room in a house or apartment and you can't seem to stop moving or to reduce the restlessness and agitation, yet you're not actually in an anxiety state.

In a small chamber with someone whose face keeps changing subtly, as if the light is playing upon it.

Alone for long periods of time, in an older hotel room or motel room.

Continually going into a bathroom or a kitchen, or back and forth from bathroom to kitchen.

Waking up suddenly from a "nightmare," or a dream about yourself having just had a different biological machine, not necessarily of the earth varieties.

Driving in a car for a long period of time.

Watching a clock that moves impossibly slowly.

In an older theater with balconies and basement, watching a film that seems familiar to you but you can't remember having seen before—usually the film will have an unusual amount of senseless violence or seem very religious, or both.

Getting a phone call in the middle of the night, especially from someone you know is dead.

Apparently attending a funeral for "someone else," . . . even more suspicious when the deceased is conspicuously unidentified . . . and perhaps unidentifiable.

Lost in a small but unaccountably complex town or a very large, accountably complex city.

Finding oneself playing with cards with pictures on them, arranging the cards in varying order; the mood is exalted, as each combination yields a new set of all-encompassing cognitions. Unfortunately, the cognitions, albeit vast and grand, don't actually refer to anything.

Inside a tunnel, ascending or descending an escalator which seems to get smaller and smaller, eventually requiring a squeeze through—head first, naturally.

In an elevator alone . . . *very* alone. And the elevator seems to be going sideways.

In front of a television set, seated in a cane, wicker or rocking chair, generally of oak, with side arm rests, unable to receive anything other than soap operas and news.

Traveling a tube while surfing.

Sitting alone in a room for a long time.

Awakening after an unusually long sleep—a full day at least.

At a discotheque, dancing to a light show and heavy metal or "rock" music—the word "rock" has a very interesting meaning, dealing with an area of basic Creation before the present cosmos was constructed—heavy metal, in the chemical sense, is a very interesting set of elements with a rapid half-life that's over before it begins.

Sitting or standing in total darkness for an indeterminate—but quite obviously long—period of time.

Standing in front of a mirror for an unusually long time.

In a city which, although large, appears to be abandoned or unpopulated.

Having strange full-blown three-dimensional, totally tactile, hallucinatory experiences of "another life," in "another world."

Dreaming you had died or "almost died."

Seeing people whom you had thought were long dead on the street or in restaurants.

Sitting in a caged area or in what appears to be a playpen for children (you will see red, blue, green, white and yellow lights just out of touching range).

Talking with mysterious strangers who stop you on a street or in a public place and begin speaking as if they know you and you know, somehow, that they do.

Feeling very tired and run-down although there is no apparent reason for it.

Feeling apprehension and intense agitation, as though something terrible is about to happen—a feeling of dread.

Getting a new car or new clothes or moving to another house or town, for no apparent reason.

Getting divorced or married or changing partners.

Changing friends or neighbors.

Listening to loud music with lots of rumbling bass sounds in it or high-pitched tones which hurt your ears.

Visiting a recording studio or broadcast station.

Leaving one country and going to another, or going from "state" to "state."

There are many more, the particulars of which can be accessed in training programs available to those learning to be professional Labyrinth Readers.

One of the first problems in dealing with the between-lives area is realizing that it's not really between lives or *re*-incarnation, but the same life lived through Creation, skipping—like a flat stone on water into the voidness of non-Creation—but the change in state doesn't change the life you're living, and ought not to affect your consciousness unless your consciousness is dependent on your actions in Samsara, the world of illusionary influences and centralized ego-reality.

When you first came into the cosmos, your idea principally was—or at any rate your hope is now—to maintain the thread of consciousness throughout your experience in the universe. Usually it works out that what with all the fascination and sudden experiences and emotional-sensory shocks, and sympathy with the focus of attention of the biological machine, and constant demands on your attention, before you realize that you're being quietly dragged into a tar-baby little by little (you rarely get caught all at once), there you are, nodding ironically, muttering something in the general direction of, "Sonofabitch! Got me again!"

We could dwell upon it—recalling in vivid, graphic detail how you got caught in biological games, but basically it boils down to the fact that you intend to liberate yourself and the universe is going to do its damnedest to stop you, and if it can't bring you to a complete stop, then it's at least going to slow you down for a while. The universe becomes like a grasping mother, a Chinese finger-trap.

For every ounce of intention you have of getting yourself liberated, there's a trillion tons of counter-intention stacked up against you.

So, what are your actual chances of liberation? Just how effective is this "Book of the Dead," anyway?

If you're looking for a teaching, it's because you've lost the thread of consciousness. One who hasn't lost the thread doesn't need a teaching—you know the whole story, and you know what you have to do about it. This leaves an interesting opening—of course, the most confused idiot will now exclaim—"Well, I haven't lost *my* thread of consciousness . . . who the hell needs a teaching? . . . I'm just flipping through the book to see if this jerk got everything straight, that's all."

Well, listen, this jerk has been through the labyrinth more times than a cat howls in heat, and if there's something stupid you can do, either in a higher or a lower dimension in the labyrinth, why, I've done it —sometimes more than twice.

There are several fundamental problems in the labyrinth. One of them is the simplest to spot and the hardest to deal with. You got so caught up in the pursuits of primate life that you're no longer interested in your prime aim as a voyager—the aim you had when you came into the cosmic theater in the first place, and now you're interested in how it all comes out and in *doing* something about it by changing the experience. You're so interested in all of that that you haven't got the time or interest to waste on all this ethereal and impractical "spiritual stuff." All right, no one can force you to practice the teachings. Maybe this time all you want to do is to re-familiarize yourself with them—not actually put them to use. So you read, study, go to a few lectures, maybe do a little hatha yoga, jogging, racquetball; if you want to go further out with it, you could change your diet, wear looser clothes, non-leather sandals, and take up transcendental tennis.

That's the first major problem of the macrodimensional domains—no practical experience during the lifetime. The middle of a voyage in the macrodimensions is one hell of a time to get your first practical experience with the teaching.

Let's say you *have* been practicing. Then what are you doing with a paperback version of this book?

Well, first of all, it's absolutely necessary to rid oneself of that pride peculiar to human primates, that conviction that we need none of this stuff because we're already there. This is just the sort of arrogant nonsense that's going to guarantee that we get knocked off in the first stages of the between-lives section of the labyrinth. Imagine someone saying to the Clear Light, "Well, as it happens, I was just a Sufi before I woke up dead!" That puts a nice neat barrier between you and a gentle blending with the Absolute, doesn't it?

The prime aim when confronted with the Absolute is to realize that you *are* the shining void . . . without losing yourself. I say "without losing yourself" to ease the Western mind, but how can you lose what can't be lost? You may lose, or consider lost, many things during that merging process, but never the essential self. The essential self may have been hidden under a tremendous load of primate conditioning, but when the biological self has been stripped off, you will see that what's real about you was never lost. Hidden under a mound of insufferable egocentricity, perhaps, but never actually lost . . . as-if lost, yes; maybe all trace of the deep self was absent every minute of your life on Earth . . . but now, finally, you can be you. Such as it may be.

The Clear Light and the essential self are one and the same, so there isn't really any "merging action" you can take, since there's nothing with which to merge, but you might continue to identify with the primate self, and feel alienated from the Absolute. The essential self has no qualities; that's how you can recognize it. One quality of the void is that it lacks any "center of gravity," or centrality. It isn't everywhere, and it isn't anywhere, but it is where it is.

Now, how can anyone possibly merge with an object of anger, fear or jealousy? And what if the Absolute takes the form, a form you impose upon it in your never-ending struggle against the unfamiliar, of someone or something you don't happen to like, or are fighting, or is threatening to you, or that you hate, or that confuses you? In other words, you had better conquer those tendencies before you attempt to merge, right?

What causes all these reactions toward "the blob" —the real world, which has become separated from the essential self by unconsciousness and considerations of differentiation?

Let's look at them one at a time, although we could lump them all together and say that these are just symptoms of your own conspiracy against yourself in that endless cosmic game called "Keep It Going."

We're going to have to get at one more item before we can discuss this situation, because we may not be talking the same language; in the text we talk about demonic apparitions, and so forth. We had better begin by defining the macrodimensional domains of the labyrinth as they are experienced between lives; it's easier without a body to see the unwinding or running-down of the consciousness accumulated in our most recent contact with the organic world and to observe its breaking apart into the primary components of life, the universe and everything.

If the voyage happens according to form—and why wouldn't it—then you'll have a very familiar and eternally recurring experience. Everything will look just the same as it has been looking—well, maybe a tiny bit more plastic and proto-type-y—*very* real and *very* ancient and *very fresh*—as if made just now, with an air of unchanging oldness . . . but if you aren't paying *very* close attention, *everything seems the same.* Of course, you're not experiencing anything different than you were during the "lifetime," but you're experiencing it *in a different way.* That's the main difference between life and death. One of the problems of voyaging in the macrodimensions of the labyrinth between lives is *familiarity* and the apparent *ordinariness* of the situation.

You'll look straight at *The Old Man* and *Mom* and talk with them about the usual things; the Old Man and Mom are going to be doing some peculiar things if you've projected familiar folks onto cosmic folks—which incidentally is the basis of organic planetary existence! Since *you* are the essential self, it's assumed by the guides that anything you're allowing yourself to experience, however discomforting and even excruciating, is all right, because they know very well that you — the essential self—are absolutely indestructible. As a voyager who is senior to any experience of reality, they rightly conclude that you have all the time there is to work out any little discomfort you might be currently freaking out about.

Now we can dwell a bit on some reactions you might have toward your "cosmic family" in the labyrinth. Your "brother" can't seem to understand what's wrong with you; your "mother" doesn't relate at all to your problems. They both trust in your eventual release from what's bothering you, but you're seeing eternity, and you don't think you'll *ever* work it out.

You feel betrayed—you were just getting used to having a biological machine and being surrounded by all that nice warm planetary atmosphere and now here you are *stripped bare* and all exposed—not just your biological machine, but *everything you are or ever were* is exposed. *They* know about you, *everything* about you because there isn't anything that *isn't* you.

It's all clear now—your lying, cheating, betrayals; you can't maintain your lies in the face of this awful nakedness . . . you're cold, confused and alone.

No matter what you do, where you go, you keep coming back to this same eternal space, because this space isn't *where* you are, it's *who* you are. There doesn't seem to be any escape, and there can't be an escape from yourself. No matter where you go there you are. You're shivering and shaking. Boy, do *you* know what's going on, and you know what's going to happen— absolutely nothing . . . nothing in the Absolute. So you become afraid, or realize that you are afraid—oh, there are some moments when it was almost all right, but never as soothing as time, space, bodies and relationships.

You ought not to expect to be able to merge with something that you're afraid of, and in this case, it's the ultimate bogeyman— you. How can you run from that? Oh—you've found a way to run from it and what do you call it? "The world"? How quaint.

Jealousy—there's a beauty. Why is it such a basic problem? Again, you're looking at these forces within your essential self as personalities with whom you've been familiar, or who have been associated with your experience of the labyrinth—in other words, you may have developed some prototype people with whom you always experience the labyrinth: the inhabitants of "your" labyrinth—the pictures through which you see your experience of the macrodimensional domains of the labyrinth experienced in between lives.

Now *he* is *in there* with *her*. Or *she* is *in there* with *him*. Or however you get that one going in your considerations. At any rate, in the text you'll notice that the fellow who comes to your rescue is always in *her* embrace—and *he or she belongs to you*. Why do you have to share *her* with *him*? Or *him* with *her*? You know that one moment in the labyrinth is at least one lifetime that they can spend with each other, all the while leaving you alone and frustrated and scared and lonely and all you want is to be held and comforted. So jealousy pops up toward *that with which you wish to become one* —in other words, to become jealous toward two aspects of yourself. This comes up a lot—this particular confrontation with a couple in union—and you might as well get used to it. This is incidentally one of the reasons for the taboo in the human sector against seeing another couple in union.

Feeling threatened? This is another major problem in the macrodimensional domains of the labyrinth. In the macrodimensions, your accumulated inclinations and tendencies as well as attachments, being out of phase electromagnetically speaking with the general field, causing a localized field-effect anomaly and all, these are picked up and vaporized by the cleansing radiations, one by one, in much the same way that irradiation reduces bacteria in supermarket vegetables. That leaves you without **any** automatic habitual functions or thought-forms to keep you going.

You have lost all of your automaticities, and now you have the option of mechanically running on, making each moment happen, pushing into the future, letting go of the present, which is to say, you find yourself faced with the necessity of creating the future moment by moment and event by event, if you're to have any time-flow at all, and that's a hell of a lot of work; so in the macrodimensions, if you're depending on an automatic time-flow, you're going to feel threatened by a static eternalized state, and you're likely to get pretty exhausted by having to manually move the hands of the clock to create the effect of a passage of time.

If you expect to be a survivor in the macrodimensional domains of the labyrinth—not escape, escape is not the object— you'll just have to practice being and functioning in the macrodimensions, getting used to all those lights, sounds and radiations, and you'll have to work on your tendencies toward anger, jealousy, hatred, violence, unconscious reaction and particularly exhaustion and fear.

Then there are your personal relationships— learning to let go of all human feelings of ownership without destroying the relationships you are maintaining in the human dimension, gaining the ability to have relationships without attachment—but with honor and integrity.

Finally, you may have a hard time *finding out that you are in the macrodimensions* until you wake up suddenly in shock, only to realize that you had been in the macrodimensional domains, but through inattention and exhaustion you have involuntarily taken rebirth in your customary human primate form, or whatever form you're currently enjoying. Perhaps a bookworm.

One way you may solve this perennial dilemma is to identify with the labyrinth guide. Don't trust your senses—everyone, anyone, everything and anything could be the guide, the Gorilla Your Dreams, the Lord of Death. Try merging with anything you come across. That telephone over there—could that be the guide? Or the TV set—is that it?

The guide may, through your tendency to convert images to the ordinary and familiar, take many forms, and has the specific function of causing and continuing the process of liberation and awakening through a series of miracles or "coincidence control." This coincidence control is also called *the grace of the guide* and includes all coincidences, like them or not, appreciated or not, in or out of awareness. Any other function or attribute of the guide is strictly imaginary. To initiate and run the process of liberation, however, one must specifically ask.

You might now see the sense of treating everyone and everything as a manifestation of God, as the mystics have said for centuries, including your own essential self, that selfness which resides deeply beyond ego, consciousness and action, none of which are actually "yours" or ever were "yours" in the sense of ownership but belong entirely to the world. You—the *real* you— exist solely as a source of attention and presence, beyond all action and involvement with the turbulent flow of biological life—itself just a secondary manifestation of localized field-effect probability and indeterminacy—all around you.

The sure way to recognize the macrodimensions of the labyrinth is to assume that you are always in them at any moment; at this very moment.

This conversation—which you seem to me to be perceiving as a message in some sort of written form . . . a book? . . . It's obvious that you've converted my presence to a safer, more familiar perceptual and experiential symbology.

Always acting as if in the macrodimensions of the labyrinth, assuming that your senses are deceiving you, will give you the necessary edge to achieve your liberation from the human biological framework of reality perception.

Your experience of the macrodimensions can be altered by the powerful habit to be human, think as a human, perceive as a human, and most unfortunately—at least in the macrodimensional sense—to *react* as a human, making the most extraordinary events and objects appear as if a normal human experience.

The reality of the macrodimensional state depends on how much attention you can bring to bear on the actual present. If you've learned to function minimally—as have most human primates—with a sort of dim permanent inattention punctuated only by an occasional shock, you're not very likely to notice the admittedly subtle differences between the organic and macrodimensional domains. It's not the *type* or character of the experience that differentiates the human dimension from the macrodimensions, but the *quality* of the experience, which is dependent upon the quality and intensity of the attention. To be on the safe side, always assume that you are presently *in the macrodimensional domains* and that your perceptions and assumptions about yourself and your environment, especially if they seem to conform to the standard human primate world-view, are completely wrong.

If you're counting on getting through the macrodimensions without any effort to learn how to deal effectively with the experience, good luck, and we'll see you back here again!

Here are a few exercises. Mostly they deal with the things we just can't allow to continue unabated in our deepest selves, if we are to continue on an upward evolutionary spiral—anger, jealousy, hunger and other masquerades for fear—we can rid ourselves of any such "hooks" we might have developed in our human experience and involvement with bodies and other biological forms as well. These hooks can really foul us up in the macrodimensions. Two kinds of exercises called "meditations" deal with these two aspects of this problem:

Type one meditation is designed to help you discover your essential self—to dig down past all the things you now identify as your self, and keep on digging down until you find the Self-Without-Qualities—this is sometimes called the "Not That, Not That, Not That . . . " meditation. You should be able to correctly identify the void-without-qualities or Clear Light as your deepest, most real self. Many techniques exist to do this—it's by far the most popular, since it goes right out the top.

Type two meditation deals primarily with phenomena—the rolling thunder, bells, trumpeting and general tintinabulous mayhem which seems to occur only during transitional phases, that is, between stable states when upscaling or downscaling in the course of dimensional voyaging; the lights are bright and dazzling, the radiation most disconcerting to the uninitiated, which is to say, to the inattentive, one who has not cultivated the fine art of intense attention. Several forms of negative reinforcement techniques and programmed responses to various chambers are an excellent safety measure against accidental rebirth. Thanks to the space-age technology of reading aloud, we now have the means to metaprogram the essential self against negative rebirths.

If you experience the macrodimensional domains as if with familiar relations, friends or relatives—common symbols of organ-

ic life as you know it—then there are going to be form changes,
face changes, reality changes—all of which could be transcendental, if you're able to go beyond human perceptual expectations.

A string of meditations called "type three" meditations are
the performing meditations—in other words, how to do something
you wish to do while conflicting realities and disorienting phenomena are running on. This type of meditation rightly belongs to
the class of phenomenal meditations, but it is not only transcendent, but active; that is to say, some action must necessarily be
taken from a standpoint beyond phenomena. These are the siddhis,
or labyrinth powers, which you can use to move yourself in the
direction you want to go in the labyrinth—something like swim-
ming underwater. Powers are not magic tricks, however, any more
than turning the steering wheel on a car. Closing the womb
entrance and choosing a womb are certainly in this third category
of meditation.

If you are curious about how the macrodimensions appear to
change and produce phenomena, it's very simple: think of a rubber
ball. On the first bounce, it has a lot of energy, so it bounces high.
On the second bounce, it bounces lower. On the next bounce, even
lower, with less energy, and so on.

At the moment of death, the voyager has most energy, so it
bounces all the way "up" into the Clear Light and, depending on
the amount of energy released at the moment of death, is able to
remain in the Clear Light for longer or lesser periods. You are
bouncing around in a spectrum of light which appears different in
color and form on each perceptual level.

On the top bounce the voyager hits the Clear Light. If the
labyrinth voyager has separated with a great deal of energy (not
fear, anger or panic, however— wrong type of energy—I mean
nervous energy) then it bounces all the way up to the top of the
Clear Light spectrum.

On the next bounce, the voyager is unable to reach as high,
this time extending only into the domain of blue light. Of course,
we haven't yet taken a look at the lower end of this. If the labyrinth

voyager is bouncing "up" into the light spectrum, then what happens when it bounces "down"? At the bottom end, the voyager bounces into a temporary oblivion. That's why, unless we are well-trained to maintain the thread of consciousness during stage-four sleep, we will tend to experience periods of blackout interspersed with periods of sudden and extreme exposure to the more intense radiation levels on the higher end of the light-spectrum, which can bring about excruciating consciousness interludes and a desire to sink into the infra-red levels of reality.

So on the bottom end, without the ability to maintain a high degree of intensity of attention and presence through the stage four sleep, the voyager will experience blackout and loss of memory, and must, through these contact readings, be reminded of what's actually happening when the light spectrum is re-entered on the top end of the cycle.

The effect is roughly:

First Bounce: Clear Light. Depending upon the amount and quality of work done on maintaining an intense special type of attention during human existence, the penetration of this field will be greater or less. Then the down-bounce into the area of oblivion. This down-bounce can be viewed as a blackout area.

Second Bounce: Blue Light. Still enough energy to escape rebirth and to attain liberation in the Clear Light; the visible light spectrum and ambient temperature plasma phenomena of the space-time discontinuum is seen from "above." The standing wave and interference patterns of the God-world seem dull white, slower, as the light is reflected and broken; the breakup points cause harmonics, following the separation of the whole-note tonic. Then the down-bounce into oblivion once again. This is called "The Bottom of the Well."

Third Bounce: White Light. Then the down-bounce again, not as deep as the first or second. Finally this bouncing up and down averages out, and the voyager is left depleted of energy, forcing one to accept submission to the all-absolute electromagnetic energy field of the lower, biological dimensions, which can be viewed as having taken rebirth on one of the six lower worlds of existence.

The real problem of primate existence is to train *not the mind, but the essential self*, the voyager, whose presence and attention survive after all ordinary forms and manifestations of consciousness have fragmented into their five basic and, to the primate mind, totally unrecognizable, components; this is roughly equivalent to a cowboy who has never been exposed to anything but duck-art and black velvet bar paintings of nude Mexican women suddenly coming face-to-face with a signed original Picasso at his most Cubist.

All the various sights you see during the voyage in the macrodimensions are simply those elements of consciousness displaying themselves one at a time, and then in merging. During the first stage of the labyrinth voyage, you see the elements of consciousness as they exist in reality. They are implacable and unchanging, yet familiar. So they are called the friendly guides. They in fact don't "guide" you anywhere, but as elements of consciousness, they do point the way toward liberation if you know how to follow them.

Then in the second stage you will see the *reflections* of the five primal components of consciousness, the "left hand of God." These are the not-so-friendly guides. As these components of consciousness merge—called "The Play of Consciousness"—one gets the effect of realities, ego, awareness, and worlds of existence and non-existence. As these components begin to merge once again, they form interlocking blendings, which can be represented by interlocked fingers of the hands—this hand-play is a special macrodimensional language called "mudra." The mudra both determines the new form of consciousness and is determined— formed responsively—by it.

The specific consciousness which forms as a result of energy loss determines how the world—which objectively never undergoes change—will appear to one in its new plasma matrix.

As the components of consciousness re-form, one seems to experience rebirth, although in fact it is not re-entry into the world, but a new construct-reality which is taking place.

Once crystallized, the newly formed consciousness cannot be altered except by a breakdown process such as voyaging in the macrodimensional domains of the labyrinth. Sometimes the reformed consciousness is even more securely programmed than the previous one, and ego is strengthened rather than broken.

This continuous process of subjective change is the only change there is. A good scientific notation of subjective consciousness alteration is the I-Ching. Another of these "living" notebooks of plasma configurations is the Kabbalah. The 99 Names of God, Mudra, Yantra, Prime-Time Programming and the Lesser Key of Solomon are further examples of change-notations in the reality spectrum.

E.J. GOLD, *FIGURE IN LANDSCAPE*, CHARCOAL ON ARCHES PAPER, 1987.

THE SIX DIMENSIONS

I enter into a dreamlike state the quality of which is like a theater in which I'm watching the creation of the whole drama of the reality of the human dimension as well as the five other dimensions of existence.

Suddenly I realize where I am. I look around and see my former selves filling the theater, all absorbed in the drama that's going on in front of them. The film is playing to an empty house. I decide to get up and leave before I fall into a deep sleep and once again, the drama catches me in its fascinating grip.

As I walk out of the theater, I can't understand how I could have fallen into that trap again and become hypnotized and stupefied by an unconnected set of pictures, and moreover, how I could have come to believe that something was actually happening to me—not only believe it, but also feel the sensations in myself as I identified with the action supposedly going on in the drama. I now realize with a sudden clarity of understanding that there is no sequence of events making up the time track and that the apparency of time is simply a random connection of pictures and sounds associated by significance to each other which only makes sense during the dream of life. I have almost awakened from the dream of existence, but the real awakening is still far before me.

Now I leave the theater and a guide rushes to help me. But I become afraid, and I try to get away from him. I don't know what to do. All I want to do at this point is to find some central anchor point at which I can orient myself, ground myself in some way. I want to hold on to something because my mind and identity as a centralized ego are starting to disintegrate.

I feel that if only I can find some point in which to center, I can maintain it. My sensations are running wild as they are no longer dependent upon a biological machine to control and buffer them. I am surprised to find that I still have sensations in this state, and my sensations, perceptions and thoughts are starting to bother me a little. I feel as if I'm at the top of a roller coaster that's about to let go, and I wish I hadn't begun the whole thing.

There is a rippling sensation of being torn apart at the seams. This is the feeling which comes from the conflict between consciousness and the biological machine which I can feel as a yearning regret and an "itchy" kind of feeling as if I have become exhausted far past my capacity, and yet I cannot rest. This is the result of the breakdown of the effort that I've been making during that lifetime to hold the ego consciousness together.

I am afraid to go insane, or afraid that I might already be going insane, but at the same time I know with the peculiar clarity of understanding which accompanies the labyrinth chamber I am in that I can never go insane or black out all the way to total unconsciousness no matter how much I might wish I could go insane in order to forget what's going to happen next.

My mind has ceased to function as it should, and my ordinary logic center has stopped working. I can no longer believe the reality of the planetary world because I see behind it now, and I know what makes it tick. But I don't know what to do, how to function, without the organic intellectual functions of the mind. I reassure myself: "Yes, I still have thoughts. Some part of my mind must still be functioning."

I become unsure of the mind, doubting its capacity to maintain itself, its ability to hold on to the structure of the ego. The surroundings become unreal and flat. I am only able now to relate to what's happening through feelings of like and dislike. This eventually gives way to a state of high indifference about it all. I give up trying to fight to hold on or to direct it, and I become fey and careless. I'm not doing it—it's doing me, so I might as well just give up and let it happen.

This passes quickly, but the guide has meanwhile had time to begin moving me toward an orientation point in the first stage of movement in the macrodimensional domains that I encounter during this phase of the labyrinth voyage, a point which I have always called "Home." This is the safe space, and once I get there I know it will be all right. I feel that I can't get there in time. I ask the guide to hurry before it's too late. The guide tells me that I am going there as fast as it's possible to go. The sensation and impression of travel is actually the passage of the sequence of events in this first stage, and so it takes a certain definite amount of time before I arrive at the safe space, "Home."

Everything and everyone in the surroundings is going flat. The whole of existence has taken on the quality of forms within a dream, and I have realized that I am now in a dream. Everything is preplanned and preprogrammed according to an unchangeable script. I now see life as only a mechanical machine without meaning or significance. It was empty all this time; there was never anyone there. None of it was ever real. All the parts were played by mechanical puppets. I was the only one in the drama, and I'm the only one who ever will be in the drama. I feel terror at the fakeness of it all. But I'm sure that I'm real and that the guide is real. And I'm headed for the only place that I'm sure will remain real even when everything else goes. But what's taking so long? Could the guide have become lost? He had better hurry! It's happening faster now.

Finally I arrive. The safe space. I rush in and there I find Her. She has been there all the time waiting for me and now I'm back. I have a faint idea to fight all this, but somehow I can't do it. If the safe space goes there won't be anything left I can depend on. So I allow it to run on. The drama is continuing, but I don't see this part as just another part of the dream. As far as I'm concerned, I've awakened to reality once again. "Help me, help me," I plead with Her. "Help you what?" She wants to know. From Her point of view there's nothing wrong. With a shock I realize that She hasn't been sharing my dream in the same way. As far as She's concerned, I've just been sleeping, that's all.

She isn't really interested in my problem. I look to her as if I'm just having some trouble waking up and am still in the twilight state. She believes implicitly that this is the awake state. She is unaware—just as I am in this state—that it is still part of the dream, just as life "down there" of "sleeping dreams" is a part of the dream. She doesn't see this state as just another experience. And He isn't much help either.

Fear is beginning to build up to a crescendo of emotion as I try to fight off waking up still further. I am afraid of losing even this little bit of ground that I have managed to hold. I still have an identity at this point. As far as I'm concerned I'm either just a human primate who has become a little confused and lost and has somehow found himself in an eternal condition, or one of the three universal gods who has been asleep and has just awakened from an unusually abrupt nap.

I feel betrayed, tricked somehow into this voyage so far beyond the seeming safety of the human primate dimension. I have lost everything I was fighting to hold on to. My consciousness is dissipating too quickly to recapture it or to get a hold on anything. It's all happening too fast for me. If only I could make it slow down I'm sure that I could stop it from going any further and bring it back the way it was. I know now that I've come to the end of the line and the beginning of the line at the same time. And speaking of time, it has stopped flowing entirely, and I'm afraid that this whole thing is going to remain like this forever, stuck in the repeating program of my asking for help and neither of Them understanding what's wrong. All I want is a little information and some help, that's all. I want them to tell me how to stop this.

I wonder whether I'm dying. My breath comes in gasps and I feel weak and faint as if something were dropping off each moment. The only flow of action is this feeling that I'm dying, and then after whatever it is has dropped off, I feel better again, as if I'm being revived only to go through it again and again. I feel as if I've been vomiting uncontrollably many thousands of times. Finally, that stage is over and I am left feeling incredibly weakened and exhausted. All I want to do right now is to lie down. But I quickly discover that I can't lie down or rest. More things are starting to happen. I find myself compulsively moving around from one point to another. The automatic actions of the macrodimensions are starting to take over and I am becoming upset because I'm losing control. During planetary life I felt as if I was usually in control. Of course now I know that it wasn't so, but I used to believe it and that was comforting.

I am losing it more and more, and the more I try to resist it the more I lose ground. Now I know exactly where I am and what's happening. This is hell. Eternally doomed to repeat this insane drama with these two implacable and unresponsive voyagers, whose only pleasure is to torment and torture me by keeping me off balance so I don't have time to think.

I try desperately to maintain some memory of my previous identity, but everything is going. I'm losing it. I wander helplessly and compulsively around the safe space which isn't so safe anymore. Now I see *them* as my antagonists. They have been doing this to me. I must have time to think. Time to think. That suddenly takes on a whole new significance as I realize once again that in order to have a mind and to create any action I must have a time track. There must be duration and connection.

In my wandering I feel both pain and bliss at the same time. I want something to happen, but I don't know what. I am looking for something. Comfort, peace, rest. But I know I'll never get down from here. On and on I go, pacing restlessly from one reference to another. From the "kitchen" to the "bedroom" to the "bathroom" to the "living room."

While I'm in the bathroom I check the mirror. I feel a rising panic as I am about to look in the mirror, but I do it anyway. It's all right, it's still me. I think of cutting my throat, but I realize that I've gone as far as possible already, and every time I've ever committed suicide I've ended up here anyway. This is where I go after I die. And I can't die any more than I have already.

The pain from the realization that I can't die hits me more than anything ever could. There is no escape from here. An intense feeling of wailing terror and regret builds up to a huge wave. With a shudder of grief I announce, "I can't die" as if for the first time. But then I remember how many times I've said it before. "It's always the same," I complain to myself.

I am in the Realm of the Hungry Ghosts, always searching for something that will make it better, but nothing ever will. It will never get any better here. This is the way this world is, always was and always will be. Since there isn't any time here, there isn't any change.

I thought that being Home was going to help me, but I had forgotten how I always felt when I was here. I am the helpless victim of an insane plot against myself. I am being forced to downscale while they laugh at my stupidity and weakness. I try once again to get them to tell me how to stop all this from happening, but they don't know either. At this point I'm so introverted into my own symptoms and sensations that I can't hear them when they tell me that they don't know any more than I do. All I'm hearing at this stage is my own truth about them and about my "Home" dimension.

The only truth I can hear now and accept is the truth that agrees with my present understanding, which is that *they know and I don't* and that *this will never end*. I begin to feel a rising panic, because I don't want to be alone, but on the other hand, I don't want to be with *them*.

I feel as if I'm stuck forever in this state, but if I am left alone I'll be even worse off, alone in the hell of emptiness and despair. I don't want to always have to be the one to make that sacrifice. I wish that there were someone else to take my place. I wish now more than anything else to be able to rest, to sleep and to dream.

Anything to have some peace from this terrible clarity. I wish it weren't all so simple and eternal.

Now I'm entering the Brute Dimension, the condition of irony without humor. It's so funny I wish I could laugh. The whole thing is absurd, but I only feel pain and fear from all this. It's been my show all the time. "Why does it always have to be my trip?" I ask them. I am unaware at this point of other aspects of the situation. I can only see my own knowledge of how it all is, my ultimate total understanding. Finally I laugh, with a short barking coarse laughter. "Of course," I admit as I surrender to it, "this is how it all is."

Now I long for the solid and predictable state of my former existence in the human dimension, back when I was still learning, exploring and developing; way back when everything was unknown and there was still something to find out; when there were paths and byways and things I had to do, and I was getting at something meaningful and wonderfully real; when it was all significant, and there were others just like me.

How nice it was when I could depend on the walls to just be solid and not breathe so disturbingly. When I had a goal of accumulating things, and if I didn't like it where I was, I could go somewhere else.

I would even settle for that life now knowing it was entirely mechanical and unreal, if only I could find some way of unknowing enough to believe in and identify with it. I wish that I could hide inside something solid, but there is nothing besides me.

I want something to prevent me from remembering this for a very long time, but no matter how long I stay asleep, I keep coming back to this and it's as if I was never gone. I want relief from reality, but I'm not sure what's real. "Real is anything you bump into," She informs me. But I know that there are an almost infinite number of realities, "wheels within wheels within wheels," all spinning inside each other in endless games within games within games. I am sure now that I will never know for certain whether I have really awakened to reality or whether it's just another dream.

I pass quickly through the human dimension because it's too painful. I've just been there, and it didn't work. I suspect that no vessel in planetary existence would be able to contain me. I experience a few hundred lifetimes now, but each one is like the passing of a single breath. There is no relief here, and so I pass out of that realm and into the next realm, still searching for peace.

Each of the three of me is trying to hold on to my own individual consciousness and existence. I play off each other. I dare not let Him be alone with Her. There is a feeling of power and certainty, and the sensations have gotten better. Most of the pain is gone, and I know I will survive and never have to fall asleep again. I feel superior to Him and yet threatened by His very existence. I juggle for position, to hold Her interest. None of me wants to be the "patsy," the sacrifice. She watches the drama go on and on, but She can't relate to it. She is fascinated with the idea of death and wonders what it feels like. Playfully She decides some more voyagers to death so that She can observe their reactions. I feel some former incarnations rise up and form within me, and am aware of their fight to remain individual and apart from me as if they had any power to struggle against it. I am not concerned with them. I'm well above incarnation and excarnation.

My companion is calmly observing me. He will never crack, and I know it. No matter what, He remains placid and undisturbed. I can't get Him to communicate. He is implacably and immovably here, and He will never change. How does He manage to stay so calm through all this? I wish I could be Him and therefore secure and solid. For a moment I change places, and I realize that I *am* Him, but I still feel afraid. I wonder whether I started out as Him or as me. "Which one did I come in here with?" I ask Him. Now I wish that I could be Her, having peace and solitude in total absorption with the dance. "When will it be my turn to sleep?" I whine. But I can't help feeling pride in being who I am, and so I hold fast to my own centralized form and consciousness. This existence will go on forever, and I am confident that sooner or later I'll learn how to handle it.

Suddenly I am aware that there are only the two of us left. One of us has merged into the others. Then just as suddenly I find myself alone once again in the blackness, floating in the electric Jell-O.

With a shock I realize that I have been chosen once again as the sacrifice, and once again I come to understand that there is no other to be the sacrifice. When it comes down to one, I'm the one.

As I fall deeper and deeper into the spinning stillness, I hope vaguely that something will happen to awaken me once again to existence, but somehow I know that nothing needs to happen to remind me that existence is just as much a part of my nature as non-existence.

I surrender to it in the knowledge that it will go on again and again over and over; and yet since there is only one Creation in one moment, it will all be the same. With a feeling of blissful ecstasy I resign myself to no change. No one will ever come along from "outside" to bail me out of it or help me escape because from here there is no "outside." For ever and ever it will always be my trip.

It is my innermost secret nature that I realize in the macrodimensional domains of the labyrinth, and the dissolution of karmic or material consciousness which dissolves in slow waves or cycles, so I feel as if I am experiencing different forms of beingness and awareness. Actually my consciousness and my beingness are always the same. Change continues only so long as I am connected with planetary existence on the six realms of experience. If I would only awaken, I could have planetary connection without sleep and experience.

E.J. Gold, *Eroica Nude*, Charcoal on Arches paper, 1987.

OBLIGATORY READER'S INVOCATION

To the divine silence of unreachable endlessness;
To the divine silence of perfected knowledge;
To the divine silence of the soundless voice;
To the divine silence of the Heart of the Labyrinth;
To the divine silence of the ancient mind;
To the divine silence of the unborn guide;
To the divine silence of the unseen guide,
    protector of all sentient life;
To the divine silence of those of perfected knowledge;
To the divine silence of human primate incarnation;
To the divine silence of the labyrinth guides
    who sacrifice their liberation for those
    who have not yet awakened to the truth;
To the divine silence of the Lord of Death,
    the eternal unborn resident of the labyrinth
who has sacrificed his own redemption
    for the redemption of all voyagers everywhere;
To the divine silence of the primordial being;
To the divine silence of the great sacrifice;
We offer homage, love and hope;
But above all, we give our gratitude.

E.J. GOLD, *MULTIFACETED FIGURE*, CHARCOAL ON ARCHES PAPER, 1987.

FIRST STAGE OF THE VOYAGE IN THE MACRODIMENSIONS OF THE LABYRINTH

MOMENT OF DEATH
THROUGH SECONDARY CLEAR LIGHT

FIRST CHAMBER

This covers the specific period between the time that the voyager or the family and friends of the voyager request readings through the vigil following Terminus. This includes getting the reader to the location of the voyager's Terminus point, confirming or altering arrangements as necessary to make the voyager's transition from the human dimension into the macrodimensional domains as gentle as possible, arranging the reading chamber space, preparing the voyager with readings and, if possible, with exercises extending into and through the initial levels of Clear Light, arranging to attend the formal service following Terminus, and making sure that the biological machine is not removed to a mortuary before a full hour has passed following medical certification of the moment of brain-death.

Step One: Terminus is close; the launch window into the macrodimensions is opening, and the voyager has entered into the final symptoms; you have already made arrangements for the cleansing fumigation of the chamber if possible . . . while incense can't be used in the presence of oxygen, essential oils can, and work as well. In some respiratory cases, of course, this will be impossible, and should be dispensed with. Flowers and candle could and should be used, if conditions permit. Generally the candle is burned and the flowers arranged, but there are no fixed rules and other options may present themselves.

Undoubtedly you have already determined the conditions under which you will work, and at the last minute, all that remains is to choose the exact location for the reader to perform the reading and to make sure that visitors remain, not too close, in an area which will not interfere with the voyager's attention nor, of course, prevent them from fully participating in the passage.

Be sure to make definite arrangements with the hospital staff and confirm that they understand the importance of not removing the biological machine during the period of Vigil, until the launch window is fully closed, and that when transition of the voyager into the macrodimensional domains is completed, you will indicate this and permit the removal of the organic remains. You should explain to hospital staff that this is generally a period of fifteen minutes and no more than half an hour from Terminus.

Most hospice staff are very cooperative and you should have no problems with this whatever. Some family members or hospital staff may wish or need to remain; carry on with your task and keep your energy and attention concentrated on the performance of the Clear Light reading.

Make certain beforehand that the hospice staff expects you and will allow you entry without having to wait at the desk for last-minute confirmation or approval from the family or doctor, unless you want to be left standing around the waiting room or lobby until a half hour after the wake.

It is your job to make certain that everyone attending and directly involved has a definite understanding of what you are going to do and what is expected of them in terms of silence and remaining reasonably still, which means not fidgeting noisily, moving suddenly or playing pinochle during the reading.

You should not allow yourself to be drawn into a defense of your actions at this time; just explain quietly that you're concentrating, you need your full attention, and that you'll be happy to explain it all after the event. The best way to handle this is to give this book to any interested inquirer . . . of course, that can get expensive . . . on second thought, better lend or sell this book to interested parties.

Step Two: If time permits, take a bath or shower and do not use perfume, cologne or after-shave, as it can be disruptive to the voyaging atmosphere. Ordinary perfumes are generally not helpful in macrodimensional inductions, and are never used by serious voyagers.

You should have set aside special clothes for voyager assistances, and these should have been cleaned and pressed, and held in reserve only for those times when you attend a voyager. You should waste no time at this, but should have had everything ready beforehand.

Step Three: Before you dash off madly to attend the voyager at bedside, it's wise to determine where the voyager is actually going to be. By the time you arrive at the voyager's home, someone may have decided to transfer the voyager to a hospital, location unknown, no note on the door, and neighbors are unaware of any of this. It is a law in many states that a terminal patient must be transferred to a hospital, regardless of his or her wishes, and kept alive with electronic and mechanical gadgetry in spite of his or her wishes to die naturally.

Step Four: Touch the right side of the frame of the outer doorway and say before entering, "Blessings upon this house in the hour of passing."

Step Five: Outside the Terminus chamber, find out exactly what the present situation is; it may have changed radically since you were called. Find out the attending physician's name, and write it down in your *Labyrinth Services Record*, the special notebook used to record all labyrinth services performed by you.

When finding out about the patient's condition, you should always determine and notate in your record book next to the exact time (times should be noted in the time column):

1. What is the voyager's present condition, both physically and mentally-emotionally?
2. What is the prognosis—how much time before Terminus?
3. Is the voyager able to communicate easily?

If there is time before the voyager is expected to enter the between-lives state, confirm all arrangements with the person responsible. Make a definite point about doing this. Many hospitals are becoming more service oriented and will try to do what you want done, but there are still some old fashioned Boris Karloff and Bela Lugosi type hospitals that regard themselves as bastions of defense of the hospital routines developed by Florence Nightingale during the height of the Crimean Conflict.

No matter what happens, don't interrupt the vigil service once begun. If problems develop with the hospital personnel, let the family take care of the situation. Don't get involved with doctors, nurses, coroners, funeral directors, or whatever. Just continue the vigil service until it has been completed, no matter what, short of being carried off bodily by grim-visaged former running backs currently working as attendants.

If you are really tuned into the space of the vigil, nothing—not even an earthquake or a former Perdue running back—will keep you from your appointed rounds.

Make allowances for the family's confusion and upsets, if they occur during and after the moments of death, and be as gentle and compassionate as possible. There is usually a feeling of unreality which occurs as a protective mechanism in the family and friends if they are under stress about death, so they will generally remain obligingly quiet under the persuasive influence of severe shock, giving you the opportunity to perform your service without interference.

Step Six: Return to the room of the patient and check to see that everything is neat, clean and orderly, but don't allow people to come in and clean it at this stage. If it hasn't been done before this, it will be too late now, and will be more of a disturbance than having a messy room to have people bustling about in there.

Waste or trash should be removed, however, and piles of books, magazines or newspapers should be removed or stacked on shelves, neatly.

Step Seven: The exact location from which the reader delivers the labyrinth instructions to the voyager is called the Ambo. A chair should be placed at the Ambo, upon which the reader will sit during the readings. If possible, the Ambo should not be moved once it has been placed.

The family may be seated behind or around the reader during the readings. Passage should be a family event, not a tragic and unknown lonely death in a cold hospital room, surrounded by weird machines—and that's just the nurses—and stainless steel bedpans.

If possible, there are much better ways to pass through transition, especially in the comfortable and familiar surroundings of one's own home, with the love of the family and friends to sustain one during those last few minutes. Until recently, this was the most common type of passage, but there's too much money at stake in hospital administration to allow this; hospitals, medicine and pharmaceuticals have become such big business in the United States that marketing to the public is no longer necessary. It's accepted by most of us that we are expected to obey a doctor when he or she tells us to go to the hospital. In a sense, we no longer have the right to choose our own medical counsel.

If they are to be used, a candle and incense can be positioned on a night table or TV table nearby. Flowers should be placed so that they don't interfere with your view of the patient. If there is muzak playing, or a music system going, or the TV is on, get it turned off . . . unless it's unplugged and running thirty year old sitcoms. Nothing particularly esoteric in this; it just makes good aesthetic sense—in addition, the reader's voice should be the only sound in the chamber . . . unless the soundtrack of *2001, A Space Odyssey* happens to be piped over the muzak system, in which case, you'd better have a good clear look around . . . things may not be quite what they seem to the inattentive eye.

Sometimes something classical, sweeping but not threatening or overbearing—Sibelius, not Beethoven, for example—may help the voyager resist panic, but generally no matter what has happened before, during the final moments, the voyager will enter into a deep, calm euphoric state, and will tend to be very lucid and receptive to the teaching, perhaps uncharacteristically in relation to the voyager's previous views.

About two minutes prior to the final symptom, even those who during their lives have been trapped so deeply within their psyches that they have been resisting it are clearly and quite suddenly able to view the levels beyond organic existence, and may, surprisingly, welcome and respond to the reading.

Many voyagers who had no previous contact with the teaching will at the point just before the final symptom, say something that indicates that they know more about the teaching and the between-lives state than you do.

It's a wonderful surprise to see the strongly resistant and inhibited psyche suddenly break down; the voyager just shines right through; with a smile, you know that the voyager is right there, and really grateful for your help; it's like a real life transformation of Ebenezer Scrooge.

Step Eight: Now the readings for the approach of Terminus begin . . . assuming, of course, that your taxi has arrived in plenty of time. If the voyager wishes, you could schedule daily or twice-weekly readings long before the big day. Preparation for the Ultimate Adventure can be extremely beneficial; it sets in good habits, which even the stress of passage might not interrupt.

When final symptoms become noticeable, stop all other readings, and concentrate on the readings for final symptoms. If the reader has not been trained in the Transference Procedures,

Confronting the Primary Clear Light and Confronting the Secondary Clear Light should be read. This provides a clear sequence of subjective impressions which the voyager will experience during the ejection phase as the biological machine shuts down and the nervous system and brain begin their final system crash.

If the voyager has had previous preparation, review the final symptoms, then during transition, indicate them as they occur.

Step Nine: When you recognize the symptoms of Terminus transition, read the *Obligatory Reader's Invocation, Readings #1-#3*, then the *Confrontation with the Clear Light*.

At this point, the voyager should be able to view all of existence as one single event, as the vision expands to include all dimensions higher and lower.

The voyager will begin to drift easily into the Clear Light, at least sufficiently to feel it as a mild electrical cushioning or warm, somewhat vibrating, descending blanket. After this relatively lucid period the biological machine will deteriorate rapidly as a result of direct exposure to the Clear Light, and transition will then be entered fully, the voyager moving completely into the Clear Light, eventually causing complete disruption of the functioning of the biological machine which will then pass through the stages of motor death, nerve system death and finally brain death.

Step Ten: Now the Vigil begins. When the voyager passes fully into the Clear Light, at this point you should read *Confronting the Clear Light* slowly . . . but not abnormally slowly . . . pausing momentarily after each sentence, using your sensing skills and monitoring your own attention—which will precisely equal the voyager's attention—to make sure the instruction got across. You may find that you are forced to depend on intuition for this.

If at this juncture the hospital staff insists that the voyager's now quite certified biological machine must be removed, don't panic. Just ask them to allow a few minutes to establish contact, then go to the hospital chapel. Almost every hospital has a chapel in it for the use of priests and family in such cases. If they don't, then ask for a space in another room. Of course, if transition occurs at home, then it's much easier, unless the family is given to extreme levels of bureaucracy.

The timing of the readings should allow for seven full unhurried readings of *Confronting the Clear Light* during the one-hour vigil. When you have completed seven repetitions of the vigil readings, stop. The next time you perform readings, they can be conducted virtually anywhere, using a photograph of the voyager.

Vigil is the most vital period of the labyrinth transition; the voyager can easily be overwhelmed at this first powerful encounter with the Clear Light and because most voyagers respond with automatic primate reflexes, this state doesn't generally last very long and the voyager passes quickly into the second stage, marked by the onset of a series of completely predictable visions. Oddly enough, although all voyagers experience the Clear Light at this point, not all voyagers are aware of it. Often the primate consciousness is so dominant, that not even the Clear Light Experience can break the sleep induced by the organic world hallucination.

The exact duration of the Clear Light state depends on several circumstances, some accidental, some not; the condition of the nervous system, organs and general concentration or dispersal of vital force within the biological machine will have some effect, but the strongest determinant factor is the degree of intensity and concentration of attention and presence the voyager has been able to develop during the few years of human life allotted for this purpose.

The voyager should take advantage of this state, because it enables one to pass easily out of the organic state, freeing oneself from the automatically proceeding influence of encounters with various bodies and biological attitudes, habits and beliefs which can be the fundamental cause of all those embarrassing little flubs in the Clear Light state that tend to dump one unceremoniously right back into the primate life down there in the lower dimensions.

Just as the voyager, when reborn in the organic dimensional levels, learns through trial and error and accumulated experience to function biologically, so also there is an awakening and learning in the macrodimensional domains, and through experiential empirical data the voyager becomes familiar with the conditions of existence in the Clear Light, if the state can be maintained long enough for new habits to form.

This is far more certain if experience in macrodimensional levels can be gained and reflexive reactions eliminated or stabilized during the human lifetime through the use of the special attention of the voyager; these methods are outlined in detail in several other volumes: *The Human Biological Machine as a Transformational Apparatus, Life in the Labyrinth* and *The Great Adventure*.

The transitional form—as a result of the extreme domination of organic habit—will at first tend to be a rough approximation of the human primate form, together with its mental and emotional sets, and this will continue through the process of separation of voyager and human biological machine, and if the power of organic karma—meaning primate habits and sense-of-self—is very strong, may persist until the moment of rebirth in the lower dimensions, which in the case of extreme organic contamination makes rebirth inevitable.

After the death of the biological machine, the reading of the *Confrontation with the Clear Light* should be continued at intervals of twelve hours—usually at six A.M. and again at six P.M.—for the next three or four days.

For a voyager who remains very attached and identified with the primate self, the Clear Light state may last about one-thirtieth of a second, but in the case of a well-prepared voyager it may continue for six or seven days, more than enough time for the voyager to stabilize a new existence well outside the domains of the Space-Time Discontinuum.

The readings should be performed as if trying to transmit over a long distance with a slightly faulty transmitter radio. In the first few moments of the Clear Light state, the voyager will probably be confused, disoriented, overwhelmed and generally too busy with the rapidly proceeding events to be able to achieve stability, so it's the task of the reader to help the voyager sort things out.

An experienced reader is able to easily determine whether a communication is being received and understood; readings are always performed as if listening to someone else reading. This receptive state tends to form a temporary bond between reader and voyager, enabling a stronger communication link.

The readings for the First Stage of the Voyage in the Macrodimensions of the Labyrinth begin on the following page.

Read the "Obligatory Reader's Invocation" aloud before each reading. A bell should be struck once prior to and then again following each instruction to the voyager printed as a reading in boldface type. This parenthesizes and emphasizes with an unmistakable sound the precise instruction for the voyager.

OBLIGATORY READER'S INVOCATION

To the divine silence of unreachable endlessness;
To the divine silence of perfected knowledge;
To the divine silence of the soundless voice;
To the divine silence of the Heart of the Labyrinth;
To the divine silence of the ancient mind;
To the divine silence of the unborn guide;
To the divine silence of the unseen guide,
    protector of all sentient life;
To the divine silence of those of perfected knowledge;
To the divine silence of human primate incarnation;
To the divine silence of the labyrinth guides
    who sacrifice their liberation for those
    who have not yet awakened to the truth;
To the divine silence of the Lord of Death,
    the eternal unborn resident of the labyrinth
    who has sacrificed his own redemption
    for the redemption of all voyagers everywhere;
To the divine silence of the primordial being;
To the divine silence of the great sacrifice;
We offer homage, love and hope;
But above all, we give our gratitude.

READING #1—The Symptoms

Waiting to pass through transition, I make the effort to release myself from the mind, habits and identity of the human primate, remembering myself as a voyager, separating myself from identification with the human primate within which I have been voyaging throughout its lifetime.

As a voyager, I release myself from the feeble grip of human primate consciousness; I feel myself reverting to my native state, the perfect shining void, endless light in infinite expansion; no past, present or future, all experience dissolving into the deep, shining eternal voidness of the void, releasing myself from the identity and environment of the human primate. I will enumerate the symptoms of transition:

1. Earth sinking into water. A deep, incessant sensation of slowly increasing pressure, of being inexorably drawn downward into a pool of mercury or lead, of melting into the earth.

2. Water sinking into fire. A sensation of clammy coldness as though one had been suddenly immersed in icewater—it begins with uncontrollable shivering, gradually merging into unbreathably hot, oppressively still atmosphere.

3. Fire sinking into air. A sensation of being just on the verge of explosion, giving way to a sensation of total dispersal of self.

4. Air into Clear Light. A feeling of being utterly at peace, utterly alone, completely outside space and time, free of all necessity; a sudden, powerful and thrilling sense of deep, ironic knowledge sweeps through the self, but this great, profound, sweeping, all-encompassing knowledge doesn't seem to refer to anything in particular.

The reader may notice one or more of the following observable indications that transition and/or the Kingdom of Heaven is near at hand:

1. Loss of control over face muscles.
2. High-pitched whistling, buzzing sounds, low rumbling thunder, or complete loss of hearing.
3. Visions, hallucinations or complete loss of sight.
4. Breath coming in gasps, Cheyne-Stokes breathing.
5. Cold sweats, teeth chattering, uncontrollable shivering.
6. Extreme agitation, anxiety, irritability, restlessness.
7. Lethargic calm, sudden inexplicable apparent absence of previous pain.

The reader should assist the voyager in the identification of symptoms as they appear one by one. When all symptoms are completed, recite in a low tone of voice:

READING #2

Now I am entering transition, and must separate myself from all ordinary material accumulations and accomplishments in my human primate sojourn; I prepare now to release myself from my human primate friends, family, home and surroundings; I can't take them with me into the Clear Light.

I prepare myself to survive transition, for I am a voyager, not a human primate; neither coming nor going, I have always remained in the here and now, although not always in the same morphology. Now my vision will be opened, and I will see that in reality it is always the same room, always the same day.

During transition, I may have some disturbing experiences, but these visions will have no power if I quickly recognize them as just the primal components of consciousness breaking up into their elemental forms.

I don't resist these perceptions, sensations and cognitions as they dawn upon me; any experience, whether apparently real or unreal, is still part of the dream, and so long as I seem to be having experiences and perceive change, I am still in the dream.

Guiding and concentrating the voyager's attention in this way can be used to attain spontaneous liberation:

READING #3

I am a voyager whose nature is in reality the Clear and Luminous Light, the Endless Voidness of the Void; I remain in the Clear Light, my soundless and motionless native state; I take my place as the eternal shining void itself. I remember the effort I made in my human primate life to exercise the special attention and presence of the voyager; I don't look for the Clear Light in front or behind; it won't be there, because I am the Clear Light itself; the Clear Light is my nature.

I don't allow my attention to wander in dreams even for a single moment; remembering myself as a voyager, separating myself from the clinging vestiges of human primate life, I balance myself between the worlds, as if I were riding a wave in the ocean. Should I lose my balance even for a moment, I will tumble into the wild maelstrom, overcome instantly by the immense power of the water.

Now I recognize myself as the shining Clear Light; remaining easily balanced in this eternal state I cannot be drawn downward into the lower dimensions of phenomena, world-illusion and organic habit.

The reader should repeat the following address (Reading #4) clearly and distinctly *at least three and as many as seven times*. To be most effective, the reader must sincerely wish well for the voyager, working with the greatest possible attention and will to bring about the liberation of the voyager. If the voyager, stripped of its ordinary human consciousness and all its accompanying intellectual data and mental mechanisms, is to recognize itself as the shining Clear Light of the void, the reader must continue this action until all hope is past. Should the voyager recognize itself as the Clear Light, it will enter spontaneous liberation without having to pass through the second stage of macrodimensional visions.

READING #4—Confronting the Clear Light

Now I am experiencing the Clear Light of objective reality. Nothing is happening, nothing ever has happened or ever will happen. My present sense of self, the voyager, is in reality the void itself, having no qualities or characteristics. I remember myself as the voyager, whose deepest nature is the Clear Light itself; I am one; there is no other. I am the voidness of the void, the eternal unborn, the uncreated, neither real nor unreal. All that I have been conscious of is my own play of consciousness, a dance of light, the swirling patterns of light in infinite extension, endless endlessness, the Absolute beyond change, existence, reality. I, the voyager, am inseparable from the Clear Light; I cannot be born, die, exist or change. I know now that this is my true nature.

The Primary Clear Light is thus recognized and spontaneous liberation is attained. But in case the reader is not certain that the voyager has attained liberation in the Primary Clear Light, the reading should be extended into the textual instructions for the Secondary Clear Light.

It can be assumed that there is now dawning on the voyager a secondary Clear Light following about half an hour after the first transition.

The Secondary Clear Light will be somewhat less intense than the Primary Clear Light.

On the first bounce upward, the voyager reaches the highest energy level of the macrodimensions, but on the second bounce the separative energies are very reduced, and so a lower peak is reached. Each succeeding peak tends to be lower as the escape velocity energy becomes less and less. Finally, as the force of energy has spent itself, the launch window into the Clear Light becomes closed, and the energy-exhausted voyager is inexorably drawn into a womb, without the means to resist. Thus inevitably comes rebirth.

When an untrained and unprepared voyager is first separated from the human primate, the former life and karmic relationships continue in the same way as before, perceptions of the environment continue in the same way, and for all practical purposes, this state of sleep and unawareness that the labyrinth illusions are beginning keep the voyager in a state of continual disorientation.

If on the other hand, the voyager has prepared for transition, the Clear Light reading ought to be instantly effective. In either case, the following reading is most helpful at this juncture.

READING #5

I place my concentrated attention on the Guide of the Labyrinth, who is the reflection of the moon upon the water, apparent and yet non-existent in itself, visualizing the guide as the Clear Light, the reflection of my own spiritual nature.

By so confronting the real nature of the guide, even a voyager who would not be expected to recognize the labyrinth without help is almost certain to recognize it. A voyager who, while voyaging in the human primate dimension, had been brought face-to-face with the Clear Light may be able to recognize the macrodimensional domains of the labyrinth just in this way.

But a voyager who knows only the theory of the method and has not experienced continual exposure to macrodimensional radiations, and practiced intentional macrodimensional voyaging and navigation may become bewildered and confused during the actual experience.

Untrained voyagers who have been during their passage through primate life become so involved and identified with primate conditioning may be unable to accept help, and in the end take a downward spiral path into helpless and unconscious rebirth.

Even the voyager who is highly skilled in the macrodimensions may, because of violence of the passage, become momentarily disoriented, thrown off-balance so much that the second stage illusions become overwhelming; for such voyagers these instructions are vital and essential.

There are those who, although already familiar with the teachings, have passed into degraded forms of daily existence, having broken vows or failed to perform their essential obligations honestly or become violent, obsessive, filled with passions and aggression. To them also this instruction is indispensable.

While in the second stage of this section of the labyrinth, one has formed what is called the radiant body of illusion, also called the "body of habits." Not realizing that the biological machine is dead, a state of clarity comes over the voyager. The instructions should be applied while in that state where objective and subjective reality meet face-to-face. The karmic pictures and the unwinding process have not yet begun.

The voyager is, for the moment, in the center of the cyclone, or more properly, the eye of the hurricane, and as the sun's rays dispel the darkness, the Clear Light and other macrodimensional radiations disperse the power of karma.

In the first stage of the labyrinth we wish to awaken and alert the voyager. If at this time the readings have been applied effectively, the secondary labyrinth visions, hallucinations generated by the unwinding of the primate consciousness, will not have begun, and the voyager has a better chance to achieve spontaneous liberation.

Repeat "Confronting the Clear Light" at 6:00 A.M. and again at 6:00 P.M. for the next two days. These are the readings for the first three chambers of the labyrinth voyage:

First Chamber: *Clear Light-clear*
Read "Confronting the Clear Light"
on the day of Terminus.

Second Chamber: *Clear Light-blue*
Read "Confronting the Clear Light"
as on the first day.

Third Chamber: *Clear Light-white*
Read "Confronting the Clear Light"
as on the first two days.

E.J. Gold, *Seated Death*, Charcoal on Arches paper, 1987.

SECOND STAGE OF THE VOYAGE IN THE MACRODIMENSIONS OF THE LABYRINTH

FIRST APPARITIONS

Read this passage before beginning the reading for the Manifestation of the Friendly Guides, Fourth Chamber of the Labyrinth Voyage:

INTRODUCTION

This is the stage in which labyrinth visions begin, during the first phases of dissolution of primate consciousness. As my voyager's attention becomes free of occlusion and identification with the human biological machine, I will see the Clear Light of the void manifesting as the face of the beloved, the unveiled vision of reality. This is what is meant by the expression "death comes as a lover."

Even though I must have missed the primary and secondary Clear Lights—or I wouldn't be hearing further instructions—spontaneous liberation is still possible, although as I downspiral, it becomes progressively less probable in this, the second stage of my labyrinth voyage.

My portion of food is given away, the body is stripped of its clothes, and prepared for the shroud, the bed is cleaned, the bedroom swept, my idiot nephew has taken over the business, my favorite Iguanacon T-shirt and coffee cup are given to the Salvation Army thrift shop, and my friends and relations are nearby watching all this and doing nothing. Well, not exactly nothing. They're cleaning us out of canapes and potato salad.

Strange, awesome and frightening sounds, lights and radiation assail me. Fatigue, terror and exhaustion are some reactions that I might feel, but if I relax, these reactions will pass.

There are six states that a voyager will experience in the labyrinth in all:

1. The state of uncertainty of the moment of transition.
2. The state of uncertainty during ecstatic equilibrium, as everything blends into unity.
3. The state of uncertainty during the experience of stark, raw reality.
4. The state of uncertainty while in the deep dreaming state during or following the Clear Light.
5. The state of uncertainty during the visionary stages, as the primate consciousness breaks apart and rebirth approaches more and more rapidly.
6. The state of uncertainty during the womb dreams, deep visionary slumbers influenced by sounds and imagination while awaiting rebirth.

There are three main stages of the labyrinth voyage: the moment of first transition and first confrontation with the Clear Light; the unfolding of the human primate consciousness into its five primal components; followed by the reformation of these five primal components of consciousness culminating in the process of rebirth.

Of these three, I have so far experienced only the first stage: the moment of first transition, deep sleeping blackout and the confrontation with the pure Clear Light of the void.

Although confronted with the Clear Light, which is a static field of intense, almost invisible radiation in what looks like infinite extension, I was evidently unable to remain stable within it and was ejected downward; it now becomes inevitable that I can expect to pass through the second and third stages of this present labyrinth voyage.

Death has now come to the biological machine, the human primate within which I voyaged through the organic world. Death comes to all forms; everything eventually is broken up by dissolution, so there's no point clinging to yet another biological form out of desire, longing for stability, or from fear and weakness.

There's no safety in the biological forms, or in anything else, for that matter. Even if I cling to the life of the primate, I won't gain anything in the long run, and eventually I'll be forced to release my grip.

It's okay to be afraid, to feel fear, but it's not okay to panic, to react to the fear. I will never struggle against fear; just let the fear remain, and keep the panic from forcing me into action I might regret.

When fear, terror or confusion overwhelm me, here is the vital secret of recognition:

Every thought of fear, terror or awe aroused by the visions in the labyrinth is caused within myself, because I have become identified with my own visions, lost in the swirling patterns of my own thought-forms; at this all-important moment of liberation, I do not become caught up in the power of my own hallucinations.

When I clear my vision the forms will vanish back into the smooth, undifferentiated jelly-like electrical field from which they came. I bring up my attention; I stop drifting into the vision state, and all hallucination will cease.

I open my vision; I allow myself to see the truth-absolute . . . a subtle, brilliant, ungraspable mirage moving across a dazzling landscape, a never-ending swirl of electrical vibration, expanding and contracting all at once . . . and yet this infinite landscape is only the reflection of the face of the beloved in my awakened consciousness.

From within the midst of this endless landscape, the natural sound of unsheathed reality comes rumbling and reverberating like the sound of thunder both distant and close. This is the sound of my deepest self, my own sound.

The body which I seem to have at present is called the body of habits, a form defined by customary morphological identity, taking the shape most comforting to me, and if I do nothing to escape automatic rebirth, surely also the shape of things to come.

But this body is not of flesh and blood, and so, whatever happens to me during this labyrinth voyage, whether in the form of sound, light or radiation—I mustn't resist; resistance to my own thought forms can cause spontaneous rebirth, since I'm resisting myself.

At this point, I don't worry about surviving. I can't die any more than I have already.

The visions which are beginning now are the thought-forms caused by the breaking apart of my previous human primate consciousness, and they're only affecting me because I am still under the influence of the organic world through long and repeated exposure to the lower material dimensions.

E.J. GOLD, *INSIDE OUTSIDE*, CHARCOAL ON ARCHES PAPER, 1987.

MANIFESTATION OF THE FRIENDLY GUIDES

Assuming I will be compelled, as is the average voyager, to encounter the full array of hallucinatory labyrinth visions as they impose their own forms upon the face of the beloved, I will try to remember that these are my own thought-forms and that they spring from my own deep consciousness.

FOURTH CHAMBER

At the moment, I seem to be recovering from a deep blackout state which occurred during my passage through the Primary and Secondary Clear Lights, but evidently I have fully recovered because it has begun to dawn upon me that I am in the macrodimensions.

As I direct my attention to the immediate environment, I recognize the familiar phenomenal aspects of what can only be the macrodimensional worlds, containing all six lower dimensions; I am aware of them, my self-directed attention sweeping over them as they revolve slowly in an inexorable swirl, emanating a deep, penetrating grinding rumble.

Now that I have recovered my full, unoccluded attention and eternalized presence, I know that any phenomena encountered here in the macrodimensions should be recognized as the primal elements which, when combined, produce the apparent effects of space and time, in which time is a function of space, and that when they separate during labyrinth voyaging, they produce definite macrodimensional effects very different from the effects of the human dimensional levels; for instance, the chamber I seem to be in at the moment appears deep blue, both atmospherically and in mood.

With my labyrinth voyaging senses recovered, I know that this is the Matrix of Space, from which all spatial phenomena arise, riddled with threads of cosmic energy, its brilliant blue radiation arousing within me a responsive element, that component of consciousness which is sensitive to, and which creates the apparency of, Space—which is to say, matter resolved into its most primal form, the etheric substance which is called light, and below the speed of light is considered matter.

From out of the heart of the beloved, a sudden brilliant, blinding blue radiation penetrates every fiber of my being, slowly and inexorably—and not particularly comfortably— burning away those automatic habits of human primate life and attachments to the organic world which have unavoidably accumulated within me through continual contamination with organic life.

At the same moment, I become aware of a soft white light which I somehow seem to know offers a refuge, perhaps a temporary relief through rebirth, the swaddling blanket of organic form, where if I allowed myself to be drawn down into it, I could feel somewhat protected and buffered from this harsh, intense radiation which burns and itches so intolerably, the deep infrared and high frequency ultraviolet rays scorching and buzzing, bursts of high-frequency thrilling through me in a never-ending symphony of raw, painful—and yet, dissolving force.

I mustn't allow myself to react to the natural fear engendered by this experience by giving in to panic and hysteria. As the radiation dissolves karma—which is to say, frees me from those results of my continual involvement with biological bodies—the ego will also dissolve, that false sense of detached self-existence generated by the human primate self, those habitual tendencies, actions and thoughts burned deeply into my essential self by slow contamination through continual contact with human primate thoughts and actions, and constant exposure to biological life.

No matter how great the fear, I won't allow panic to rise so much so that I am helplessly drawn down into the soft, pleasant seductive white light, because I know that once engulfed by the lower dimensions, I'll be pulled into rebirth, overwhelmed by constant distractions, forced by attractions and repulsions to wander in sleep through all six domains of organic existence, and I may not have the opportunity to escape this powerful wheel of karma for a very long time, and with this vision, I am given strength to resist rebirth by the realization that ultimately, here I will be once again, faced with the same dilemma; to give in to the soft, seductive light of rebirth, or not to give in to panic, to accept the brilliant and dazzling blue dissolving radiation without resistance, to welcome it and bathe myself in it, in the mood of gratitude, as it dissolves away every last shred of habits, attitudes and occluded human primate vision.

> When wandering in the six lower dimensions
>   because of the power of habits,
> Bathing in the brilliant radiation
>   of the matrix of space,
> May my essential self, the voyager,
>   be cleansed and guided by the inexorable
>   wisdom of reality,
> May the Beloved be my protector,
> May I be brought safely across
>   the shocking ambushes and sudden,
>   unexpected vistas of the labyrinth,
> May I be brought to the liberation
>   of the pure shining void.

Concentrating my powerful voyager attention in this way, arousing in myself deep feelings of intense humility and faith in the unchangeable nature of reality, remembering that I cannot change what is, but I can learn to like it, I allow myself to merge and become engulfed in the halo of rainbow radiation, the heart of the beloved, the seed of all universal forces, the realm from which there is no return.

FIFTH CHAMBER

In spite of this direct confrontation and concentration of attention, through the power of violence, anger or simple but stubborn obstructions of human primate conditioning, I have evidently been so overwhelmed by illusions that I remain helplessly caught up in the unraveling visions of primate life.

Dawning upon me now is the primal element of pure form, emanating suddenly from the heart of the beloved and piercing my own heart; a white, luminous and brilliant radiation; with my labyrinth voyager senses recovered, I recognize the basic components of consciousness which when combined produce what is called the element Water.

I see before me the face of the beloved, surrounded by a brilliant white radiation which emanates from the heart, bathing me in a harsh, biting acid-like cleansing atmosphere, purifying me, dissolving away all vestiges of violence, anger and hatred, all those fear reactions which remain from my voyages among humans in the primate dimension, and at the same time, I'm aware of a soft, seductive smoky light offering refuge through lovemaking and rebirth in the hell-dimension.

I could run from the dazzling, painfully annoying white radiation, but if I do, I accept rebirth in the hell-dimension.

I realize instantly that I must not allow anger and hatred to well up in me; dissolving habits of anger, those automatic biological reactions which my ego creates to hide its humiliation that it feels fear.

This knowledge that anger is a reaction to fear gives me strength to liberate myself from rising panic; I need not protect myself from humiliation; with this understanding, I am able to allow the brilliant white cleansing radiation to dissolve every last shred of anger and hatred accumulated from contamination with the life of the human biological machine.

I can safely and gracefully bathe in the dissolving radiation without fear, allowing it to wash away aggressions, not resisting the purifying process.

I feel the inexorable power of the soft, magnetically seductive path which leads to violence and anger; I must not allow myself to fall into it, or it will be my destiny to be reborn in the dark side, the hell-dimension, that domain in the lower dimensions which is formed by violence and anger.

If I give myself over to the dark side, I am destined to endure unbearable torture, pain and misery, with little hope of liberation; without resistance, I will not allow myself to be drawn down into lovemaking by the soft, seductive smoky light which is the collective force of fear and anger; I collect my attention and bathe myself in the brilliant, dazzling white radiation; holding my attention rooted upon the white radiation, I form and concentrate my thoughts in this way:

When wandering in the six lower dimensions
    because of the power of violent anger,
On the radiant path of the mirror of wisdom,
May I be guided and led
    by the guide of the labyrinth,
May the Beloved be my protector,
May I be led safely across
    the shocking ambush
    of the voyage in the labyrinth,
And may I be placed in the state
    of the pure and shining void.

If I concentrate my attention in this way, with humility and faith, I will merge into the rainbow light of the heart of the Sun-Absolute and attain to complete union in supreme blissful happiness.

SIXTH CHAMBER

Even when confronted in this way I may experience obstructions from karma, and may not be able to confront my situation because of pride, even though I am being offered the chance to be drawn away from the dangers of the labyrinth by these dissolving radiations. I may try to strike against them and run away to hide somewhere. If that happens, then the bringer of beauty, along with the light from the human dimension, will appear.

The primal form of the element Earth is going to shine outward like a yellow radiant beam. At the same time, the yellow aura of the Great Mother, absorbed in the total meditation of zero interest, zero attention and zero information, descends upon the beloved, altering the visage and mood.

This phenomenon is always accompanied by a rainbow of light, and sure enough, I'm not disappointed this time, either. The primal form of feeling and sensation manifests suddenly from the heart of the beloved, dazzling and brilliant, dripping with spheres of yellow radiation so clear and brilliant that it hurts to look directly at it.

A brilliant yellow radiation strikes and although I know it's coming before it hits, I'm still surprised at its harsh and savage intensity. At the same moment, a soft blue light opening the path toward the human dimension also strikes my heart and begins to tug at me, trying to draw me down into a lovemaking scenario in the human dimensions.

If I have any egoism of the human primate left, any pride at being anyone in particular I may be afraid of the brilliant yellow light, because it does tend to dissolve all egoism, including mine . . . .

I may be inclined to escape its presence, to try to get out of the way, to run, to hide somewhere to avoid it. The soft blue light of the human dimension will seem like an attractive and safe place to hide compared to the immediate threat of the powerful yellow radiation, but I must not be afraid of the dazzling yellow light but let it hit and strip me of ego. I will know it to be wisdom; keeping resolved to trust in it earnestly and with humility. As long as I recognize it to be the radiation of my own essential self, I still need to make efforts to be humble. If I can focus my attention on the radiant face of the beloved and allow the harsh yellow radiation to do its dissolving work, I will find myself merging inseparably with the Voidness of the Void, and will in that way attain some measure of eternal liberation.

If I can't recognize the radiation of my own consciousness, then I must arouse feelings of humility and as much faith as I can muster in the face of helpless mirth. Focusing my attention, I concentrate in the following way:

The radiation emanating from the beloved is the grace of the guide of the macrodimensions; I will take refuge in it. It is the purifying force which dissolves my attraction to the lower dimensions; by this dissolving radiation I can remain free from the compelling power of human life to which I am drawn by long-established habit; I must have faith in the cleansing radiation and accept its help.

That soft blue light of the human dimension is the path of accumulated tendencies of pride and arrogance, reactions of fear to fear; they are the cause of an enforced sense of self-egoism; if I allow myself to be engulfed by it, I will experience rebirth once again into the human dimension, needlessly suffering the same old routine; birth, childhood, an endless round of daily drudgery punctuated by grimly entertaining weekends, followed by forced retirement, old age, sickness, death and finally, here I am again.

I might become trapped in the human dimension. That's an obstruction on the path to liberation, so I should immediately allow the brilliant and dazzling yellow radiation to do its purifying work; I bathe in it, rejoicing in my newfound freedom.

> When wandering in the six lower dimensions
> because of the power of pride and ego,
> On the radiant light-path of the wisdom
> of harmonious equilibrium,
> May I be guided and led
> by the guide in the labyrinth,
> May the Beloved be my protector,
> May I be brought safely through
> the shocking ambush of the labyrinth,
> And may I be placed in the state
> of the pure and shining void.

If my attention is concentrated and clear, I will merge into the heart of the beloved, in a halo of light called the rainbow-bridge, and attain completion in the region known as Endowed-with-Glory.

SEVENTH CHAMBER

Having thus confronted the visions of the labyrinth, however weak my attention may have been until now, I ought to have gained liberation by now, unless my abilities toward higher development may be so lacking that I have been unable so far to recognize reality. Obscurations from desire and stinginess may well have placed me in a condition of helplessness and awe, too weak to resist the urge to hide from the rumbling, grinding sounds and harsh dissolving radiations.

If that has been the case, then the visage of the element Fire, along with the soft yellow light of the dimension inhabited by hungry ghosts proceeding from greediness and insatiable hunger for things, attachment to objects and possessiveness toward accumulations of things, will form upon the face of the beloved.

I will listen closely to the sounds, keep my attention sharp and clean, not allowing myself to be drawn downward into the ten thousand distractions of organic life.

My attention rests firmly on the red aura around the beloved, the primary component of perception. I see the beloved now as the eater of poison, wildly seductive and wickedly compelling, filled by the presence of the Great Mother, surrounded with a swirling halo of rainbow light.

The brilliant red dissolving radiation explodes out of the heart of the beloved, penetrating my being, and alongside that explosive red radiation is another light, the soft yellow pathway leading to the dimension of hungry ghosts, they who are never satisfied.

If I still feel possessive and attached, as I was conditioned to feel in the human primate life, I may be afraid to allow the dazzling red light to dissolve my habits of attachment and possessiveness.

If I cannot rid myself of the need to hold on to my attachments, I'll feel warmly attracted to the soft yellow light, which will seem to be a safe haven from the brilliant red radiation. I must not allow myself to be drawn into the soft yellow light, while at the same time allowing my tendencies toward attachment and possessiveness to be dissolved in the cleansing radiation, resigning myself to freedom from desire, thus allowing my unencumbered self to become engulfed inseparably into the void.

If I find myself unable to allow myself to be cleansed in this way, then I can concentrate my attention in this way:

> This is the dissolving radiation, and even if I succeed in avoiding it now, it will always be with me wherever I go, and will always be facing me when I return this way again; therefore, I won't allow myself to be drawn down into the soft yellow light, the path leading to the dimension of the hungry ghosts.

If I become attached to the soft yellow light, and am drawn into it, I'll be born into the dimension of hungry ghosts, and experience unbearable hunger and thirst. No matter how I fulfill myself there, I will never be satisfied. I will be continually hungry and at the same time full. I won't have an opportunity to attain liberation in this condition, so that's obviously an obstruction on the path. I can let go of habits and tendencies to have things and to accumulate and hold on to possessions, and allow the brilliant red light to do its work to draw me away from the dimension of hungry ghosts. I will concentrate on the beloved who appears before me, forming my thoughts in this way:

When wandering in the six lower dimensions
     because of the power of intense attachment,
On the radiant light-path
     of discriminating wisdom,
May I be guided and led
     by the guide of the labyrinth,
May the Great Mother be my protector,
May I be safely led across
     the shocking ambush of the labyrinth,
And may I be placed in the state
     of the pure and shining void.

By concentrating my attention sincerely and with humility, I will merge into the heart of the beloved, in a rainbow bridge of light, and attain completion in blissful happiness.

EIGHTH CHAMBER

Even though primate conditioning, habits and tendencies have been so long established that I wasn't able to let them go, and the occlusions of terror, egoism, greed and jealousy have all failed to be dissolved by the cleansing radiation and I have wandered this far, there's still something that can be done to get myself out of this inevitable downslide toward the lower dimensions of the labyrinth.

Now the guide of the element Air, the Almighty Conqueror, along with the dissolving radiations of his grace, will appear along with a light coming from the angelic dimension proceeding from the passion of jealousy.

The green light of the primal form of concept will shine toward me. At the same time I am aware that the green aura of the Unborn Balancer of Almighty Power, seated on a floating throne has descended upon the form of the beloved, who is filled with the presence of the Great Mother, surrounded by a rainbow of light.

The primal component of consciousness called "concept" will shine as the green light of wisdom, dazzlingly green, transparently clear and radiant, beautiful and terrifying, surrounded by globes of green radiance. Coming out of the heart of the beloved will be a shock of brilliant radiation. I remain calm and clear, remembering myself as a voyager and not a body and mind, bathed in a state of high indifference and high attention.

Along with the brilliant green radiation I feel a soft red light coming from the dimension of Purgatory. It is produced from the tendency to feel jealousy toward others, and the habitual desire to engage in intrigue. Repulsion and disgust, even deliberately aroused, will only make it worse.

Since the brilliant green radiation dissolves all tendencies of jealousy, I may view it as a threat if I feel unable to function without jealousy and envy; the radiation may terrify me and make me want to run, but the only place I can hide is in lower dimensions, so I won't try to hide from it. That soft, seductive red light is going to look pretty inviting and safe just about now, because it will allow me to hold on to my jealousy, but I won't give in to it; I recognize the brilliant green light as my ally, as wisdom itself.

Letting go of my struggle against its work of dissolving my tendencies toward jealousy and envy, I bathe in the grace of the beloved, forming my attention in the following way:

I rejoice in the dissolving radiation; even if I try to withdraw it will follow me since it's a part of my own nature. I don't want to drift into the soft red light of the lower dimensions. The light of the lower dimensions is the accumulated path of intensified jealousy. If I become attracted to it I will be reborn into that dimension, and will constantly have to protect myself by intrigue and spitefulness. Obviously that's another obstruction in the path of liberation, so I should avoid it. I let my tendencies of jealousy be stripped away by the cleansing ray of green light.

Wandering in the six lower dimensions
    because of the power of jealousy,
    on the radiant path of light
    of the all-performing wisdom,
May I be led by the guide of the labyrinth,
May the Beloved be my protector,
May I be led safely across
    the shocking ambush of the labyrinth,
And may I be placed in the state
    of the pure and shining void.

If I have concentrated my attention sincerely and with humility, I will merge into the heart of the beloved in a rainbow bridge of light and attain liberation within the voidness of the void.

NINTH CHAMBER

No matter how compelling my karmic connections, no matter how powerful my desires, I should by now have been liberated by all these confrontations with the dissolving radiations; however, if I have been exposed for a long time to habits and tendencies in the lower material dimensions and I'm not familiar with this process and have no desire for wisdom to burn away attachments, then I may be led toward rebirth by the power of negativity and violence, in spite of these many confrontations and all the help I've been offered so far.

The dissolving radiations might not have been able to burn up all my karma just yet, and I could still wander spiraling downwards because of feelings of confusion, terror and awe generated by exposure to the lights, sounds and radiations, and the threat of being stripped of attachments to a familiar reality or central egoistic reference point.

Now all five orders of dissolving radiations, together with all six lights coming from the six lower dimensions, will appear at once.

Until the last change, each of the five orders of guides appeared one by one, and I tried to confront them and accept help from them, but because of tendencies toward customary attachments, jealousy, anger and distrust, I was afraid of them and have been down-spiraling.

If I had recognized the radiations of the five guides to be the emanations of my own thought-forms, I would already have attained completion by having been absorbed through a rainbow bridge into the heart of one or another of the forms of the guides.

An enormous explosive crescendo of lights called the "lights of the union of consciousness" (composed of the combined forces of space-and-voidness, form-and-voidness, feeling-and-voidness, phenomena-and-voidness, perception-and-voidness, and concept-and-voidness) will appear all at once. I will welcome them and not be afraid of them. At the same time from the central realm of the expanded seed, which I can see from where I am, the beloved is with me, all around me and within me. There is no difference between me and my perceptions.

By now I should have questioned whether I want to return endlessly to the life of any biological machine, no matter how seductive, and decided that to cling to organic corruption is worthless and gains me nothing in the end.

So having regained the knowledge of the eternal voyager, I have further pondered over my attachments to touch, feeling, sensation, self-will, cognition and desire, and discovered that all phenomena is illusion.

Now finally my attention gives way to a state of emptiness which in turn becomes the pure feeling of ecstatic futility, which in turn leads me to the fully collected state of total attention on the voidness of the void.

Now upon the visage of the beloved I see in rapid succession the faces of the four door-keepers: each of which signifies respectively perfect compassion, benevolent mercy, ruthless love and objective justice.

Now I am aware of the presence within the beloved of the Guide of a Hundred Sacrifices; the Lord of Warfare; the Lion; the One with the Mouth of Flame; and the King of Truth. In the exercises I must learn to recognize them. The All-Beneficent Father and the All-Beneficent Mother, the Great Ancestors of All, will also appear. These perfected individuals who serve in the labyrinth as guides appear, and as an experienced voyager, I know them for what they are.

These presences arise from within my own essential self which, including the central part, make up the five houses of the voyager. All these issue from within.

The changing forms of the beloved exist within the eternal endlessness of my own primal consciousness, and I recognize them for what they are also.

The guides of the labyrinth present themselves in response to necessity, not to my necessity but to the necessity of the totality; these guides are formed into groups of five pairs, each group of five being surrounded by a circle of radiation; the male guides taking on the nature of the Divine Father, and the female guides taking on the nature of the Great Mother. All these divine forms will radiate in one complete common-presence. These are the visible forms of accumulated experiences in the lower and higher dimensions of the labyrinth, the forms that have appeared on my path who have helped me toward my own awakening, and I should recognize them as crystallized impressions.

Now from the heart of the beloved the dissolving radiations of all four wisdoms, extremely clear and refined like spider's threads, extend through the matrix of space like shimmering rays, passing through cosmic bodies as though through nothing.

Now the white light of the mirror of wisdom, transparent, glistening and dazzling, beautiful and terrifying, made even more dazzling by the surrounding globes of transparent lights, each like an inverted mirror, will shine upon me.

These radiations will all explode toward me and strike my heart simultaneously. I can't be hurt by them.

All those are the reflections of my own essential self shining. They haven't come from anywhere else or anyone else. They're mine and mine alone. I won't become attracted to them or feel weak or afraid. I will remain in the state of passive interest, in the mood of a man witnessing his own biological machine drifting down-river without trying to grasp it or to stop its motion. I won't break the natural flow of reality with thoughts.

As I remain in the non-attached state of the experienced labyrinth voyager, all forms and radiations merge within me, and with me, and thus I attain eternal liberation from the distractions of matter and energy, free to carry on the eternal battle against the forces of good and evil.

Having become familiar with the unchanging truth, I have produced in myself the tranquility of the expanded state, and having merged into the body of the perfectly evolved essential self, allow myself to be engulfed by the heart of the labyrinth, the placeless place from which there is no return.

Along with the radiations of wisdom, the soft and seductive lights of the six lower dimensions will also appear. They are a soft white light from the dimension of the gods, a soft red light from the dimension of angels, a soft blue light from the human dimension, a soft green light from the brute dimension, a soft yellow light from the dimension of hungry ghosts, and a soft smoky light from the hell dimension. Thus these six soft, seductive lights will appear along with the six radiations of wisdom, but I won't be attracted to the six lower dimensions of the labyrinth. I will just allow myself to rest quietly in the mood of high indifference.

If I allow myself to become drawn downward into lovemaking by the soft, diffused and seductive lights of the six lower dimensions of the labyrinth, then I will assume a biological machine in one of these dimensions and suffer its miseries.

Therefore I bathe myself in the dazzling pure dissolving radiations, realizing that the compassionate radiances of the wisdom of the heart have come to take hold of me through compassion. I will take refuge in them, and I won't yield to the illusory lights of the six lower dimensions of the labyrinth. I devote my complete attention toward the guides of the five orders of the heart, and concentrate my attention in this way:

Alas! when wandering in the world
    through the power of lust,
    hate, stupidity, pride and egoism,
On the bright radiance-path
    of the four unified wisdoms,
May I be guided and led by the five
    victorious conquerors of reality,
May the five orders of the Beloved
    be my protectors,
May I be rescued from the attractive
    and compelling force
    of the soft, seductive light-paths
    of the six lower dimensions,
And having been saved from the ambushes
    of the dreaded labyrinth,
May I be placed within the five pure realms
    of the divine.

By focusing my attention in this way, I can recognize my own essential self and merging in objective reason during at-one-ment, attain completion. Through faith and love and hope, the ordinary individual can come to know himself and attain his liberation. Even the lowest and most impure person can by the power of sincere and humble concentration, in all purity, close the doors of the six lower dimensions and by gaining an understanding of the real meaning of the unified four wisdoms attain completion as the supreme personality of the void.

And so by these confrontations I am destined to be liberated. I will come to recognize the truth. Many attain their liberation in this way.

If I have accumulated heavy negative karma, having no thought or liking for any teaching or prayer, or have failed in my life-purpose or vows, through the power of illusion, having not recognized the truth although confronted by it so many times in the last several days, I might still feel drawn toward rebirth.

TENTH CHAMBER

Now voyagers who hold knowledge will appear. At the same moment, the pathway to the brute dimension, the dimension of stupidity and passion for ignorance and unknowingness will open up and try to attract me.

The multi-colored radiation of the pure tendencies will shine and at the same time the voyagers who hold knowledge will appear.

From the center the Lord of the Dance, the supreme holder of knowledge who ripens karmic fruit, his aura radiating a rainbow of color, his form filled with the presence of the Great Mother, the mother of the cosmic sky, will appear.

To the south, the holder of knowledge called He-Who-Has-Power-Over-Duration-of-Life, whose aura is yellow in color, smiling and radiating light, filled with the presence of the sky-mother, will appear. To the west, the guide called the Holder-of-Knowledge-of-the-Great-Symbolic-Gesture, whose aura is red in color, smiling and radiating, filled with the presence of the Great Mother, will also appear.

To the east, the holder of knowledge called Dancer-In-The-Flame whose aura is blue in color and whose being is filled with the presence of the Great Mother will also appear.

To the north, the guide called the Self-Evolved-Holder-of-Knowledge, whose aura is green in color, with a half-angry, half-smiling and amused facial expression and whose form is filled with the presence of the Great Mother, will also appear.

There will also be a great number of female guides of the places of cremation, of the three abodes, of the thirty holy places, and of the twenty-four places of pilgrimage, of the heart center, the throat center, the brain center and the places of worship, also heroes, heroines, warriors, protectors of the faith, both male and female; and sounds so immense as to confound and confuse one with their unbelievable roaring and crashing and booming. These deities will either receive me and help me or they will try to overwhelm me for being caught up in illusions.

Also at this time a five-colored radiation, emitted simultaneously from the purified and perfected tendencies, vibrating and dazzling like colored spider threads, flashing, radiating and transparent, beautiful and terrifying all at once, will emanate out of the hearts of the Five-Chief-Holders-of-Knowledge so strongly, shockingly and brightly that I may not be able to look at them.

At the same time a soft, seductive green radiation coming from the brute dimension along with the rays of wisdom will appear.

Through the influence of my karmic tendencies toward envy I may want to hide from the rainbow light of wisdom, and I may also feel attracted to the nice, harmless-looking, soft, seductive green light coming from the lower brute dimension.

From the center of the brilliant rainbow radiation, the sound of the shining Clear Light will reverberate like the sound of a thousand thunders. This sound will come with a rolling reverberation which will sound like a mob of millions of insane hunters screaming "Kill! Kill!" Chanting will seem to come from everywhere. It's just my own consciousness creating significance where there is none. Those sounds are just what they seemed to be at first: rolling thunder.

I won't become attracted to the soft, seductive green light of the lower brute dimension. If I become attracted by it, I'll be pulled into rebirth in the brute dimension where stupidity is the practice, and I'll have to suffer the misery of slavery to a population of morons who practice treachery and brutality as a matter of course. Their treachery and brutality are made even worse by the fact that they are totally unaware of their brutality. It might be a long time before I can get out of that one. It isn't a good place to hide, and only if I really have a desperate urge to hold on to my karmic tendencies toward envy and spitefulness will I feel that it's a safe space in which to hide from the brilliant rainbow light.

If I'm having trouble, then I can concentrate my attention in this way:

> All these guides have come from the dimension of Purgatory to receive me and to help me through the labyrinth: I invoke their presence: up until today even though the five orders of guides have all exerted their compassion and dissolving radiation, I haven't been able to allow myself to be helped by them. Have pity on me! May the knowledge-holding guides not allow me to keep downspiraling any further than this, but hold me up through their compassion and mercy.

Collecting myself, I'll concentrate my attention in this way:

> O you knowledge-holding guides,
>   please listen to me;
> Lead me on the path,
>   with your great love and compassion;
> When wandering in the labyrinth
>   because of these
>   intensified karmic tendencies,
>   on the bright light-path
>   of the simultaneously-born-wisdom,
> May the guides lead me,
> May the Great Mother be my protector,
> Rescue me from the shocking
>   and fearful ambush of the labyrinth,
> And help me achieve completion
>   in the real world.

If I have concentrated in deep faith and humility, and my attention was clear and pure, there is no doubt that I will be born within the Sun-Absolute after being merged in a rainbow-bridge of light, into the heart of the holders-of-knowledge.

Having now fallen to this lower stage of the labyrinth voyage I must look to the dimensions of embodiment, rather than to the Sun-Absolute as places of refuge. Although liberation into the void can be attained from any form of existence, I may not be able to reach it unless I can restore my depleted death-energy with energy self-generated. Since most individuals are not trained to do this, I should assume that I had better make the best of the situation as it is.

Anyone coming to recognition at this stage can attain liberation—even those with the heaviest negative tendencies. This ends the method concerned with confrontations with the friendly guides of the first path of the second stage.

E.J. GOLD, *LION-HEADED WOMAN*, CHARCOAL ON ARCHES PAPER, 1992.

MANIFESTATION OF THE UNRESPONSIVE GUIDES

Read this passage before beginning the reading for the Manifestation of the Unresponsive Guides, Eleventh Chamber of the Labyrinth Voyage:

These are the visions of the unresponsive guides, immediately following the visions of the friendly guides. I must remember that I can achieve liberation at any moment just by the power of recognition, penetrating through these visions into the Clear Light, from which they have come and back to which they shall return at the moment that I am able to recognize them as products of my own consciousness and imagination.

Through powerful attachments, dense occlusions and negative emotional habits, tendencies which have been in force for a very long time during my latest exposure to lower dimensional animal bodies—especially human primates—although confronted with the full impact of reality in all its wealth of presence and immense detail, I find myself engulfed in the inexorably compelling and magnetically seductive descending spiral path.

The next phase in this descent will be continued unwinding or unraveling of consciousness, going backward from the sequence in which it had accumulated in the human primate consciousness, but now at a far more accelerated pace which means that the visions are going to continue, but on a more intense and discomforting level; after gathering energy, the storm which has let up for the moment is about to resume again, at its fullest fury.

I must remember that these visions are exactly the same as those which passed before, because I'm voyaging through the same domains as in the previous pass, but the aspects of these visions will change somewhat, due to the increased momentum of the unraveling process, as well as the fact that I'm viewing them from a much lower energy level in relation to the level on which I saw them before.

But even though they may seem different to me now, I know that these are the same domains as before, and that nothing is going to happen to me that hasn't happened before . . . and yet, here I am to tell the tale.

Because these visions are all just the reflections of my own fear and fascination, they are more resistant to dissolution through the power of recognition.

To reduce their power to overwhelm, all I need do is invoke within myself the highest possible attention and presence, and at the same time, recognize all visions other than the pure Clear Light of the void as projections of my own deep consciousness.

If I can accept the visions and sensations of the macrodimensions without resistance, even though there may still be fear and confusion, knowing that all apparitions, sounds, lights and radiations are projections of my own consciousness, that they are in reality no more than swirling patterns in the living energy field of infinite light, then they can have no power to overwhelm me.

My aim should be to achieve immediate spontaneous transition into the highest possible dimension, complete and stable transition into the pure undifferentiated presence of the living void, or at worst, conscious rebirth within the body of the teaching.

I remember from my previous experiences in the macrodimensions that this is one of those times when I'm not going to be able to take a moment's rest, because no sooner does one change cease than another begins, and since the space is eternal, there's no time flow, and therefore no end to it except by upscaling or downscaling through the macrodimensional levels.

In a very short time, the changes may be too compelling, too fascinating not to watch, and my attention could, if I lose the intensity and force of my attention even for a single moment, become enraptured and fall quickly and deeply into the bottomless well of apparent reality.

However, rather than trying to withdraw my attention, I know from previous experience in the labyrinth to use it, and even to intensify it, to penetrate the visions, diffusing them once again into the smooth, swirling patterns of the Clear Light to which they belong.

As for the untrained voyager . . . well, no point even mentioning that unfortunate being, because the vision of the unresponsive guides is going to blow the unskilled macrodimensional voyager away, right over the edge into the lower dimensions . . . no doubt about it, the self is the ultimate bogeyman.

On the other hand, a voyager with practical skill in the science of labyrinth voyaging will easily recognize these cold, deadly and unresponsive apparitions as projections of the accumulated world consciousness of the by now thoroughly deceased human primate which was left behind.

I allow all feelings of fear to pass through me, merging with all visions, liberating myself from the apparitions and entrapments of the lower dimensions.

When abbots and metaphysical doctors who give lectures and discourses experience transition, if they have remained uninstructed in the practical art of macrodimensional voyaging, it doesn't matter how strongly they held to their religious practices and how clever they might have been.

Among human primates they might have been accepted as scholars and great beings, but in the macrodimensions they're just another unskilled voyager destined for rebirth.

For such unfortunate creatures skilled in life and unskilled beyond life, the rainbow halo will not be visible at the funeral pyre nor will bone-relics emerge from the ashes.

When they lived in the human dimension, the mystic doctrine of the labyrinth never dwelt within their hearts, and because they never allowed themselves to be initiated into the actual practice of the teachings, they have accomplished nothing which transcends human death.

Even someone who has delivered ten thousand learned lectures on labyrinth voyaging, won't be able to survive the power of the visions now; the most highly disciplined monks, priests and doctors of metaphysical discourse, if they haven't learned to exert the necessary intensity of attention both concentrated and diffused, are destined to enjoy rebirth in the lower dimensions.

When the visages and emotional auras of the unresponsive guides are superimposed upon the beloved, I must remember to recognize them as my own projections, and not to view these face changes as foreboding evil, danger or antagonism; if I react in repulsion, I may find it difficult or impossible to blend my own energy field with that of the beloved; but if I am able to merge with the guide at this point, I should be able to thus liberate myself from the endless action-reaction game maintained by our opposing and unblending vibrations.

Those who have developed great proficiency in the visualizations need not descend into the lower dimensions; if they are able to accept death as a lover, then as they offer their last breath to the lover, they are drawn up directly into the Clear Light.

As a sign that this has happened, the sky may become cloud-less, followed by sun-showers, and the sweet smell of atmospheric incense, faint music, radiant phenomena, and other phenomena of passage occur at the passing of a great being as transition is achieved.

And so, to the scholars, abbots, priests and doctors of philosophical discourses, and to those mystics who have failed in their vows, and to all ordinary human beings, I offer this method, and for those who have learned to increase the intensity of the attention and who have learned to quickly and easily recognize the Clear Light at the moment of transition, and most importantly, to accept the guiding spirit of death as a lover, these readings provide all the clues necessary for one's own liberation and for the eventual liberation of all beings everywhere.

Recognizing the Clear Light even now during these visions of the unresponsive guides as they play across the face of the beloved, insures that even if I do happen to descend into the lower dimensions, I will be born into the teaching in the next rebirth.

If I can manage to awaken my attention, and can accept the full reality of the macrodimensions, the divine state of liberation should dawn upon me as the cycle of death and rebirth is broken; I will then have in my own power the option to return voluntarily to the human dimension in the awakened state, there to labor for the benefit of the Absolute.

Should recognition be delayed even momentarily, a partial awakening but not the full, unclouded realization of the unshrouded Clear Light is attained, but even with a partial awakening, I will be reborn on a macrodimensional level and soon will be brought once again into the study of labyrinth voyaging, from the precise point that the study was interrupted in the previous organic world sojourn.

So then, this is a method for entering into liberation, guided by the sound of the readings toward the pure, clear,

almost invisible dissolving radiations which burn away the habits of the organic world which still may cling to me after my journey in the material world, and which cleansing allows me to then take the secret path.

The method for macrodimensional voyaging combined with the *Invocations of Power* and the *Confrontations* will help me to voyage with the fullest possible attention, producing the greatest possible waking state, the least occlusion of the whole of reality, and the least possible resistance to liberation.

So now I am prepared for my first confrontation with the unresponsive guides of the labyrinth as their visages play over the face of the eternal beloved.

ELEVENTH CHAMBER

Up until now, I have been unable to penetrate and dissolve these apparitions into the endless undifferentiated Clear Light, and so I now enter the domain of the unresponsive guides; I will remember to recognize them as my own projections onto the face of the beloved, and will not allow my attention to wander or be distracted.

Along with these new visions, I have become aware of a distant high-pitched whistling sound; invisible radiations are beginning to penetrate my presence, but I know that I must fully relax and allow them to do their work, because in reality these are the cleansing radiations, which dissolve all accumulations of biological habit and attitude, allowing me to accept spontaneous liberation by merging with the beloved, becoming the whole chamber, turning my gaze both inward and outward at the same moment.

Above all, at this moment, I must not give in to the urgent distress which I feel, nor try to communicate with the visions of the unresponsive guides whose faces I see superimposing themselves over the face of the beloved; I know them to be completely implacable entities who are incapable of response; I know that any response I do happen to evoke, will be utterly nonsequitur and unrelated to my prompting, however connected it may seem.

I observe without negative reaction that all my actions, thoughts and beliefs are perfectly reflected by mimicry; this is the vision of my own simulated self-image in the harshly perfect mirror of pure timeless space.

TWELFTH CHAMBER

If I allow my feelings of fear to give way to panic, then the visions of the unresponsive guides are certain to appear again.

I must try to recognize the forms I see before me as embodiments of my own deep consciousness. I remember the teaching: it's all right to feel fear, but not to panic.

This vision I see before me is just another projection from my deepest consciousness; at this macrodimensional level of the labyrinth, I am the only one; there is no other. With the dawning and acceptance of this all-dissolving truth comes instantaneous liberation.

THIRTEENTH CHAMBER

Occlusion and identification with the primate self of my most recent incarnation reinforces my animal habits; strong biological feelings and thoughts have accumulated within me, urging me to seek some refuge from these dissolving radiations which strip me of my former self, and my reactions have invoked the visage of the Master of the Order of the Precious Gemstone who appears now in a flaming halo of light, his self-luminous and terrifying form rippling over the dim, subtle form of the beloved, his dark hand enfolded over a clear black gemstone, emanating a dark light hypnotically drawing me down.

But I am not drawn down; quickly, without resis-tance, I recognize this apparition to be the embodiment of my own sleeping attention, a vestigial remnant of my voyager-experience among human primates, all of which will soon be dissolved by the cleansing radiation which thrills through me now and, allowing my presence to diffuse through all forms in the chamber, I am free.

FOURTEENTH CHAMBER

Now, in this low place, I can see that, through the power of negative tendencies and habits of primate life and organic sleep I allowed feelings of panic to rule me, reacting to my deepest fears and feelings of irony and profound dismay, and that because of this, the guide of the Order of the Lotus has emerged from the Western Quarter of the labyrinth, taking a dim, sinister shape over the face of the beloved, separating us as a mask separates the face behind the form.

I make the conscious decision to thoroughly enjoy this apparition, recognizing it to be the projection of my own expectations here in the macrodimensions; as an experienced labyrinth voyager, I know not to react suddenly, no matter how startling, unexpected or repulsive the apparition; as recognition of my own thought-forms dawns upon me, liberation also comes.

Through acknowledgment of this vision as my own projection out of my own deepest consciousness, I blend easily and gently with the beloved, merging in full at-one-ment, inexorably absorbed into the void, achieving the stable state of liberation from all visions of the void.

FIFTEENTH CHAMBER

Despite these confrontations, I still find myself in a spiraling descent through the macrodimensions toward organic rebirth; yet I know that it is still possible to achieve liberation if I am able to resist the urge to run away and hide.

I will not allow my attention to become confused or distracted by anything that seems to be going on.

At the moment, the unresponsive guide of the Order of Karma will spring from the Northern quarter of the labyrinth, superimposing its form and visage upon the beloved; I take care not to react to my feelings of fear and dismay; I know that I can't be overwhelmed if I recognize this entire event to be a projection of my own consciousness.

Since this vision is my own self-teaching experience projected by my own deep consciousness in the form of a full-blown tactile hallucination, there is no reason to react; I simply acknowledge it as my own and thus become able to merge with the beloved, liberated from all visions which cause repulsion and attraction.

Through the teachings I have learned to recognize the guides as pure thought-forms emerging automatically from my own deep consciousness. No matter how grotesque and terrifying these apparitions may be, I am able to recognize them as my own and they quickly lose depth and resolution, dissolving and receding into the formless Clear Light of the void from which they came, holding no further power over me.

SIXTEENTH CHAMBER

Through the power of apparitions produced by the habits accumulated in my human primate life, I have reacted with fear and repulsion, and therefore the previous confrontations have failed to produce liberation.

I know that now the eight chaotic evil forms, each having the characteristics and personality of an animal, will emanate from the eastern quarter of my deepest consciousness, hovering like wraiths upon the face of the beloved.

I know them as my own projected thought forms, taking shape before me, and I allow the feelings of fear and betrayal to pass through me as cleansing radiations, freeing me from all resistance to the beloved, merging into at-one-ment now, dissolving the primate self back into the void from which it came.

I now notice the presence in the chamber of a powerful female force, intensely studying visions of warfare and destruction; she listens and watches with total fascination and equally total unconcern; it is obvious as I observe her, that she has never suffered pain nor tasted death.

I sense her longing for suffering and death, which she can experience only by watching and listening; she is so obviously fascinated by death, suffering, warfare and murder, and delights so in the destruction of flesh, that I know clearly that I am in the presence of that macrodimensional being called the Great Mother.

I feel myself surrounded by female forces of great mystical power; those who find fascination in horror; the female guides of the organic dimensions.

These eight female guides, emerging from my own deep consciousness, cause no fear in me; I recognize them as my own thought-forms, and feel love for them, and cherish them as they take shape over the beloved; so deeply do I engulf them in love that I dissolve into them and through them merge into the heart of the beloved, thus liberating myself from this vision and all visions in and of the void.

SEVENTEENTH CHAMBER

Now the four female gatekeepers and the four keepers of the keys will spring out of my deepest, most unreachable consciousness, appearing in solid image projection over the form of the beloved.

From the east quarter of my deep consciousness, the white auraed prodding goddess will transform the beloved into something ferocious; now the shape shifts again as from the southern quarter, the yellow auraed goddess descends upon the beloved; from the west, the red aura of the lion goddess alters the face and distorts it horribly; from the north, the green aura of the snake goddess gives a terrifying aspect to the face of the beloved; quickly I recognize these form changes as just the visual hallucinatory play of my own deep consciousness, and their significance fades away as they dissolve gently into the swirling patterning shadow-show of the empty void.

Now as more female guides overtake the beloved, the face twists and distorts, grimacing menacingly, smiling horribly, a fearful specter of death; I quickly recognize them as manifestations of my own thought forms, and as my vision penetrates through them toward the beloved, the fear-inducing apparitions recede into the void from which they came.

The face of the beloved grows grim and grotesque as from the north is evoked the blue auraed wolf goddess, then anger swells and the mouth sneers angrily as the red auraed ibex goddess descends upon the form; now another grotesquerie, and yet another, disfigures the face of the beloved and turns my heart cold with fear, and brings the fainting weakness of dismay and terror as the black auraed sow goddess, the red auraed crow goddess, the giant goddess and the blue auraed snake goddess, each momentarily superimpose their horrible visages, dark emotional auras and chaotic temperament upon the form of the beloved.

But all the while I keep myself gentle and receptive, remembering that these wild, chaotic, sinister visions are automatically produced by my own deep consciousness, and through this recognition and acceptance of them as my own, they dissolve immediately into the featureless landscape of the empty void, allowing me to merge into the heart of the beloved.

Whereas the friendly guides are the active emanations of the void, reflecting the primordial unshaped tranquility of the voyager, the unresponsive guides are the passive emanations of the Clear Light inverting itself within the disruptive electromagnetic field of the time-space discontinuum.

And now the unresponsive guides who hunger for worldly existence impose themselves as objects in the surroundings, but I am able to recognize them by their presence and awareness; they watch me and speak silently to me; bringing my attention to full intensity, I see them clearly, and knowing them to be projections of my own consciousness, I permit them to melt into the featureless void, at the same moment, allowing myself to be drawn into the heart of the beloved in the perfect state of at-one-ment, thereby liberating myself from the power of all illusions.

My thought-forms are exposed as apparitions, yet if I lose the force and intensity of my attention, I allow myself to be overwhelmed by the experience, wandering unknowingly and stripped of my will, into the lower dimensions.

I now recognize all existence, all phenomena, to be an automatic projection of my own deep consciousness, but I seek redemption now simply by merging with all visions, all apparitions, all radiances into the heart of the beloved.

I seek no refuge from the terrifying visions, shapes, sounds and radiations, knowing and recognizing them as self-projected images, and even as all the guides from all quarters of the labyrinth blend together to form the terrifying apparition of the Lord of Death, I penetrate my vision through my own intricate illusions, recognizing my own thought-forms by the use of the art of the invocation of my own presence and attention, and by the power of one sound, I merge with the beloved, attaining spontaneous liberation in the heart of the labyrinth.

They come to me now, visions of bitter, hateful, vengeful creatures, snarling and biting with frustration, their glassy hypnotic stares seeing nothing, their angry ears hearing nothing, eating meat and drinking blood but tasting nothing, their hunger unabated, filling the world with their excrementa and repulsive presence.

When these thought-forms dominate my consciousness, I won't be afraid or overwhelmed by them; the body which I now possess is an immortal body of karmic tendencies, and so is simply a form of accumulated habits acquired in long association with the biological machines in the material worlds, and even though run through with a sword or cut with a razor or chopped to bits, it cannot die. Because my body is in reality a body unborn and uncreated, made up of the voidness, I don't have to be afraid or keep trying to protect it from harm.

The shapeshifting forms are hallucinations generated by my own deep consciousness, the stuff of which dreams are made; voidness cannot destroy voidness, and somewhere beyond the lights, sounds, terrifying forms of the Lord of Death, the beloved waits for me to overcome my fears, merging in at-one-ment, with no resistance to reality.

Knowing this, all terror, fear and doubt dissolve; I feel relief at recognition of the great truth and thus attain liberation in the supreme moment of self-surrender to the shining luminescence of the void.

> Wandering in the labyrinth,
> I have become lost and confused.
> Uphold me by thy grace, my beloved;
> I am wandering, lost in the labyrinth;
> Rescue me! Don't let thy grace forsake me!
> Through the force of overpowering illusions;

On the path of light of the abandonment
   of fear, anxiety, fright
   and being overwhelmed;
May the guides lead me;
May the goddesses of space and time
   be my protectors;
Save me from the shocking and fearful
   ambushes of the labyrinth;
Help me to regain the power
   of my presence and attention
   so that I may merge with the beloved
And be one with the shining endless void!

When wandering alone,
   separated from my dear friends,
When the forms of the voidness
   of my own thoughts are shining upon me,
May the guides exert the force of their grace
   and help me to be unafraid,
   without terror or awe,
And remain awake in the labyrinth.

When the five bright lights of wisdom
   shine upon me here,
May recognition come to me without dread
   and without fear of being overwhelmed;
When the divine bodies of the friendly
   and unresponsive guides shine upon me,
May I receive help to remain without fear,
   and to recognize the labyrinth.

When the power of karma causes me to seek
   the refuge of suffering and misery,
May the guides dissipate the longing
   for misery and suffering
   which has come upon me;

When the sound of reality,
　　the objective world sound,
　　reverberates like thunder,
May it be transmuted into the sounds
　　of the six karma-dissolving syllables,
"Om-Ma-Me-Teg-Mi-Om."

May these six syllables bring one into the real world and close the portals of rebirth in the lower dimensions; "Om" among the gods, "Ma" among the angels, "Me" among humanity, "Teg" among the sub-human heavy-jawed creatures, "Mi" among the wandering, insatiable hungry ghosts in the spirit world, and "Om" among the inhabitants of the living hell.

When unprotected in the labyrinth,
　　stripped of will-power and forced
　　to follow my karmic tendencies,
I invoke the compassionate one of grace
　　to protect me here;
When suffering the miseries of karmic habits
　　and automatic mechanicality,
May the blissfulness of the Clear Light
　　dawn upon me;
May the five elements,
　　the primary-light-formations,
　　not rise up against me as my enemies
And may I not see them as enemies;
May I instead behold the perfect visage
　　of the beloved,
Merging into at-one-ment with the void,
Beyond all forms, apparitions and visions.

I offer this attention-concentration in sincerity and humility; I know all fears and terrors will disappear and liberation will be attained without doubt. This is important to remember and to perform correctly with genuine good wishes and sincerity. The quality of sincereness is the most important factor here.

Being undistracted by anything proceeding within me or around me, I concentrate my effort and attention on this concentration recognizing the beloved behind the illusion, merging now in at-one-ment.

I know—I have always somehow known—that just behind even the most solid, implacable form, behind all the attention-demanding events of life, all the grotesque, unsatisfying sexual contortions of matter and energy, somewhere behind that grinding, writhing wall of flesh, that grinning mask of death, if I can only discover the means to dissolve it, to penetrate beyond it, the beloved waits patiently while I grope blindly for the key that opens the door of solid form.

E.J. GOLD, *LOOKING BACKWARD*, CHARCOAL ON ARCHES PAPER, 1987.

THIRD STAGE OF THE VOYAGE IN THE MACRODIMENSIONS OF THE LABYRINTH

REFORMATION OF CONSCIOUSNESS

Read this passage before beginning the reading for the Third Stage, Re-Formation of Consciousness, Eighteenth Chamber of the Labyrinth Voyage:

PRELIMINARY INSTRUCTIONS

This book of rebirth presents my instructions for the selection of a suitable womb and for closing the womb entrance should the womb prove unsuitable.

In choosing rebirth, the higher my being as a voyager, the less likely the choice of a couple in passionate or aggressive lovemaking. A very experienced voyager will regard any passion or off-centered sexual ego-game as an unsuitable womb.

I can choose a suitable womb by non-movement, calm and centered emotion, controlled breathing of the couple in embrace, the scale of beingness of the couple—easily discernible in the lucid knowingness that a voyager possesses when in the macrodimensions of the labyrinth. The depth of the meditation of the couple and the degree of reverie are also visible to me from a voyager's point of view in the labyrinth.

The method of choosing a womb is made easy by my increased and clarified state of knowingness in the third stage of the voyage through the labyrinth. The method of choosing a particular lifetime is made easy by the beloved, who presents the options for my development as a voyager through various lifetimes.

My real difficulty in the third stage is to close the entrance to a womb into which I do not wish to enter.

My primary effort in the third stage is to be able to recognize a suitable womb, because perceptions are confused and wombs seem to be other objects entirely.

Instructions in the third stage are intended to close the entrance to an unsuitable womb, to provide the data and impressions which enable me as a voyager to discern the difference between one womb and another in one or another dimensional level.

So begins the instruction for the third stage of the voyage through the labyrinth:

E.J. GOLD, *NUDE IN THE BIJOU THEATRE*, CHARCOAL ON ARCHES PAPER, 1987.

CHOOSING REBIRTH

GUIDING IN: THE SELECTION OF A WOMB

EIGHTEENTH CHAMBER

It has been difficult for me. I've been asleep during all of this and got into the belief that it was all happening as if true. I have just completed a guided tour of myself, composed entirely of the primal elements of my own beingness.

Each of the visions or cognitions I've had is simply one or another of the basic modules of consciousness itself. When I suddenly found myself in the macrodimensions of the labyrinth, I realized that I had fainted for a few days and that I was able to function with supernormal clarity of understanding. I discovered that I had an apparent form similar to the one I've been used to as a human being. I am Adam, the son of Adam. This body will never die no matter what happens.

> With all the senses intact,
> Wandering through endless endlessness,
> I now have the power to change the dream,
> Being both the dream and the dreamer.

Even though the voyaging form can't die, that doesn't mean it can't feel pain. This body has sensations, just as the biological machine had. Since it doesn't have a threshold for pain as the biological machine did, it allows even more sensation—perhaps more than I thought I could ever bear. After a while I suppose I'll get used to it which isn't too likely, as my consciousness is rapidly enough getting ready to cram itself into rebirth.

If my consciousness forms into a god ego, I'll be born in the Sun-Absolute. If it forms into the ego of a guide, then I'll be born in the dimension of Purgatory, and so on, depending on chance, influences of habit, luck, accident and the odds. I am going to be hearing a lot of sales pitches on the merits of various lifetimes, and I'll have to make a decision rather quickly, so I must be prepared. Once it starts happening, I won't have a chance to reconsider. Depending on my inclinations, desires, beliefs and tendencies, I'll probably end up likely as not with some sort of compromise. The usual response to the question "What do you want to do now?" is "Anything but this," and with that sort of undefined answer, that's what I'll probably get.

Whatever visions dawn upon me, I won't allow myself to be drawn into a state of desire, which would cause inexorable rebirth in one of the six lower dimensions.

NINETEENTH CHAMBER

The magnetic forces of rebirth are starting to take hold because I haven't yet recognized that all these experiences and cosmic cognitions I've been having are just my own consciousness unfolding and folding and that every vision was formed from the basic module forms of my own beingness.

I relax, allowing myself to be the pure luminous non-located void in a state of non-action, without trying to reach for or withdraw from anything or hold on to anything I think

I need in order to stabilize myself; I thus am able to attain spontaneous liberation even at this stage of the game, and I won't have to be reborn in the lower dimensions.

If I'm still having trouble realizing that all this is my own consciousness taken apart piece by piece and displayed for my enjoyment and indifferent amusement, then I'll visualize the beloved or my teacher in the human dimension floating above me, and get into a state of non-attached devotion toward him.

It's very important that I make some effort at this stage to resist rebirth as my temporarily macrodimensional will is stripped from me by the inexorable process of rebirth. I won't allow myself to wander off that meditation. I'll feel lethargic and apathetic at this point, and I'll want to give up.

Surrender was a good idea back a few days ago, but now it's not the thing to do. I'll hold on and try to regain my sense of humor about this whole situation.

TWENTIETH CHAMBER

My present form exists without limitations; I find that I can move easily through all areas of the reality spectrum, viewing all aspects and details of all six lower dimensions as I wish. My movement seems to be directed by the power of my attention, and places me in that locality of the space-time discontinuum.

That can actually work for me at this point, because by simply listening to these instructions and allowing these sounds and concepts to direct my attention, I move to the areas pointed out as desirable, and move away from those designated as undesirable or counterproductive to my evolution as a being.

TWENTY-FIRST CHAMBER

The beloved asks me where I want to go, what I want to do. I want to be attentive, not to automatically respond, "I don't care—anywhere but here." Instead I indicate my wish for liberation in the pure realm of the Clear Light, and if this isn't presently possible, then at least a good rebirth in which I will be able to work on myself in this teaching. If I give in to my tendency to run away from the guide or from the strange sensations I'm getting right now, then I'll get a random rebirth based on karmic accumulations and habits.

I can tolerate it long enough to get a good rebirth. Even the sensations of the two-headed room can be tolerated for a few moments. I will continue to concentrate on rebirth in the realm of the pure Clear Light, or at least a rebirth in which I am in a position and condition to learn and practice the teaching, so this won't happen again as badly the next time I pass through the macrodimensions.

Freedom of movement through the six lower dimensions is a positive sign that I am in the stage of re-formation of consciousness, which is called rebirth.

At this time I'll remember what I learned in the teaching while in the human dimension. Now I have supernatural powers to alter my place in reality. I won't depend on or become absorbed in these powers. They are simply powers to alter the dream in one way or another, but they don't change my situation or beingness. In fact they can make it worse by disguising reality in a way that maintains the illusion. If I use them now to try to escape from the macrodimensions, I will just trip down another primrose path to yet another dead end.

TWENTY-SECOND CHAMBER

I may begin to see those who are going to be reborn with me, and I hold myself clear of the desire to be with them by concentrating on the beloved instead.

In this state and with this macrodimensional consciousness form and superacute attention, I will now see my family, friends and home of the last lifetime as if I were there with them once again, but no matter what I do or say, they won't respond, and trying to get them to respond may get me into a worse condition than I am in already. I'll let go of any idea of influencing them or communicating with them. I might be feeling regret at the loss of all that I had accumulated in that lifetime, but it's important right now to let go of all that I once was or believed myself to be. I can't hide there anymore.

My path is now strongly set for rebirth, and I feel driven by a powerful wind behind me. That's the wind of karmic desires, inclinations and tendencies and is nothing but my own attractions and repulsions about existence.

It all seems so ordinary and familiar, like some eternal "déjà vu," and yet at the same moment somehow unutterably alien, unpredictable and strange. I will imagine that I am being hunted like a wounded animal, and I'll hear sounds of "Get him!" and "Kill the sonofabitch!" I won't be afraid of that; it's just my own paranoia that those against whom I committed what I consider to be negative acts will take their revenge on me while I'm vulnerable.

I feel disaster. Visions of earthquakes, floods, fires, or the explosion of hydrogen bombs assail me, yet I know that these anxieties are nothing more than the automatic results of my organic habits imposed upon me during my previous exposures to organic life, producing what are still extremely powerful and active reverberations of aggression, passion and ignorance within my partially re-formed consciousness. As this begins, I direct my fullest possible attention in this way:

Please don't let me forget
  what's really happening.
Don't allow me to fall into sleep once again.
If you can't get me out of this,
  at least get me to a good rebirth
Where I can work on getting rid of this
  unconscious ego
And learn to be myself.

TWENTY-THIRD CHAMBER

If I have been practicing the teaching during my life in the human dimension and have accumulated baraka, or grace, I won't have such a bad time of it here. I'll be feeling rather blissful and pleasant right about now.

But if I have been indifferent toward the teaching during life I will now see indifference and ignorance all around me. If I see objects of pleasure and desire, I won't try to go after them or bring them in to me. I'll offer them to the beloved instead. I'll give it all away to the Office of Coincidence Control. I will let them have it all. I realize that none of this is real enough for me to actually possess anyway.

I'm in a state of indifference to it all. I won't meditate on forms or try to visualize at this point.

I'm about to take the Grand Tour of Safe Spaces, shelters of refuge. I'll see all sorts of nice safe buildings, tunnels, caves, shrines, temples, monasteries, palaces, rocks, trees and boxes. Anything solid and safe-looking is going to attract me now. These wombs are all traps. I may want to become a bronze statue or hide inside a rock. But I won't give in to the temptation.

TWENTY-FOURTH CHAMBER

I don't seem to be able to hold onto or stabilize my fast and fleeting consciousness at this point. My thoughts are coming more and more rapidly, and I seem to have unaccountably lost the ability to make any sense of how they string together or what their sequence means.

Everything seems isolated and disconnected, all out of context. I'm feeling hungry and tired, don't want to run or wander, feeling as if I'm about to be caught and captured. All I want to do right now is hide inside something.

The idea of getting into rebirth in an undesirable or miserable lower dimension is the cause of this desperation to find a safe space in which to hide. If I don't panic, I won't get rebirth in a lower dimension.

On the other hand, if I become desperate, I may try to squeeze in between some rocks or buildings, and in fact none of the safe spaces I'm seeing are actually as they appear to be. Those are wombs in various dimensions. They're color-coded; I can look carefully at their color and I'll be able to tell which dimension I'm being attracted to.

TWENTY-FIFTH CHAMBER

At this point I'm likely to feel that I'm about to be the victim of some kind of attack, perhaps hunters, or a killer who's after me, or a coven of evil witches trying to destroy me with electrical spells, or federal and other espionage agents closing in on me, or the bogeyman waiting behind some door or in a back corner to gobble me up. But the fact is that it's my own show. No one is trying to do anything to me. I'm being driven and haunted by my own thought forms and paranoia.

If I'm still convinced that any of this is other-determined and that I'm the victim of a bad case of pantheism, then I'm now going to perform one of the dumber actions of this voyage, and not without some pride.

I now recall and recount all the things that I consider good that I've done, and then all the things that I consider bad that I've done, and compare them for the benefit of the beloved, who is now accommodating my desires by appearing and acting as a judge. Feeling very intense and serious while I'm justifying all these actions, I may feel that these are my own actions which I initiated, unless I can recall the mechanical nature of the world, and that through constant exposure to its distractions, I have become convinced that I'm a definite ego with a will of my own, with the ability to alter action in the world, and the ability to do something other than what's happening.

The beloved will now be pretty threatening to me, gently inquiring if anything's wrong. I'll shake and shiver. I'm sure I've done something wrong. I know that if I am too egotistical to admit cleanly and clearly that I'm afraid and don't know what's going on, I will be compelled to go through the next little drama:

I'll protest that I haven't done anything wrong, and then suddenly all the things I consider to have been wrong actions that I've taken will appear. All my fears are now about to come true. That old eternal buddy, the beloved, is suddenly going to accommodate my present impression by assuming the form, feeling and visage of the Lord of Death, the Monkey Man, the "Gorilla my dreams," the Crazy Clown; we look into the mirror, or the fire—however I see the cosmic computer—and it points out that I need some punishment, which I've known all along.

At this point I'm going to get exactly what I expected. If at this point I realize that this is just my expectation and that my karmic tendencies are bringing all this about, then I could be spontaneously liberated right here and now.

If on the other hand I am really heavily identified with this drama, then the next step is inevitable. After all, why shouldn't I be the effect of it? Isn't this what I've been doing to others all this time?

The Monkey Man is going to tie me up with a rope made of my own guts and drag me around. Then he's going to cut my head off, tear out my heart, pull out the remainder of my intestines, drink my blood, eat my brains, skin me and eat the flesh, and then gnaw on the bones. And if this isn't enough, he'll plague me with bad puns all the while he's doing it.

TWENTY-SIXTH CHAMBER

It's happened to me again. Unfortunately this body is immortal, so no matter how many times that happens to me, I'll recover, but even though I can't die, I can feel exquisite pain. If I had only realized that I am the shining and luminous voidness, none of this would have had to happen to me again.

TWENTY-SEVENTH CHAMBER

After I get the punishment I think I deserve for being such a rotten being, a great emptiness, as if a huge weight had been lifted from, will come over me. This isn't a negative emptiness, the absence of somethingness. It is the ever-empty endlessness which is the awe-inspiring quality of the void. There has never been anything within the void. It has never been filled with anything that now has been emptied of some-thingness. It has always been the void and always will be the void.

If I am able to view the emptiness as it is, as my own deepest self, my own nature, then I will be able to cross the great desert and be instantly liberated. This is the point of no return, the macrodimensional crowbar which separates the sentient voyagers who are liberated and those who take lower rebirth.

In one single instant they are parted from one another; in that instant, infinite freedom or the wheel once again.

TWENTY-EIGHTH CHAMBER

If I'm still in the process of degenerative rebirth, I've obviously allowed myself to become confused by all the shadow show going on around me, afraid and overwhelmed by it all. If I give up now and fall asleep, I'll be carried downward, out of any chance of liberation in a macrodimensional domain. But beyond this point, I won't be able to attain spontaneous liberation just by pure recognition, because I'll be too buffered for recognition to have the same power to liberate me.

If I can't handle it here, I'll just remember the beloved's form and visage as that of a pleasant and safe being who wants to help me get free of this. I'll tell my real name, and thus be liberated. Now I am going to be tossed around between states of joy and sadness alternating in each moment. I won't get caught by trying to resist with aggression and I won't give in to blissful sleep through passion.

TWENTY-NINTH CHAMBER

If I am going to be born in one of the higher realms and my relatives or friends are doing something stupid such as sacrificing animals, or something that's equally ignorant, I won't feel anger or express resentment toward them or try to get them to stop doing it. I'll just let them do what they're doing and be what they're being. It's here, under pressure, that I'll see just how non-attached I really am. If I feel any anger or resentment toward their displeasing manifestations or ignorant thoughts, I'll be drawn into the hell-dimension and will be born as a hell being.

THIRTIETH CHAMBER

If I'm still attached to any of the people or possessions I left behind, or if I feel attached to the power I had there, and get angry or upset about it, that will cause me to be drawn to the dimension occupied by hungry ghosts or to the hell-dimension, even if I was just about to be born in a higher state. It can cost me very dearly to be attached to anything I left behind.

Even if I am attached to the people or things I left behind, I can't have them any more anyway. I can't get to them. That whole reality is behind me and I can't get into it now—I've outgrown it. If I'm having trouble letting my attachments go, I can give them as a present to the beloved; let the beloved take them and give them away for me. That way I'll be able to let them go more easily. I'll try to remain in a state free from desires. I know that I don't need or truly want anything.

THIRTY-FIRST CHAMBER

While the readings of this book are going on for me and I watch through the ethers, as a result of impure thoughts and perceptions arising from my karmic tendencies, I may see the readings being done carelessly, stupidly, sleepily, inattentively, without any real intention or interest in my condition, and I will feel the lack of faith and feelings of fear or disbelief in those who are reading for me. I will feel that they have betrayed me, and I will become upset or angry at them for not performing these actions correctly or well enough. That will send me to the hell-dimension or the dimension of hungry ghosts as sure as death and taxes.

If I become upset with them for not performing these functions well, I'll have forgotten that this is my trip and they are simply acting out parts in my drama!

I am observing the community of beings of pure spirit and thinking that they are my personal friends and that I've been watching the pure shining luminous nature of the void, and if those folks are doing anything wrong, it's because I have them doing it.

It's important to make the assumption that, no matter how I'm seeing it, everyone is acting and performing on a very pure level and that no matter how it seems to me, they're practicing pure devotion.

THIRTY-SECOND CHAMBER

It may have become apparent to me by now that there are three different types of perception or awareness in the macrodimensions.

On the first stage, the point of creation, I can treat the visions exactly as they appear to me. On the second stage, the point of destruction, I can trust the visions to behave as if true, also. But on this third stage, creating the absence of the creation, I can't trust the visions to be as they appear, because they have been created to hide or disguise something. As an example, there is the story of the hungry monk who found a leg of lamb, but just as he was about to eat it, the green guide came up to him and told him to mark it with an X. The next day the monk found an X marked upon his own arm. The visions here are of the same quality. I can't assume that anything I see is as it is.

In order to avoid birth I will have to either recognize that anything I see is in fact the shining luminous void and nothing else, or I'll have to decode the real meaning behind each of the images I see.

THIRTY-THIRD CHAMBER

I begin to feel as if I'm being pushed from behind toward various spaces or objects by a steady and compelling force.

I feel as if I am being hunted by something horrible. The beloved will look like a gorilla, or a fierce animal, or a pack of hunters or perhaps an insane blue-eyed red-haired clown. I will feel that I have to escape, that I have to find some place in which to hide.

If I know the visualizations, I can transform the hunter into the beneficent and friendly beloved of the macrodimensions, seeing all phenomena as simple apparition without any real nature of its own other than the power I give it.

I'll let the vision dissolve slowly from the edges inward and meditate on what is left after it is gone. I apply the emergency attention-concentration for closing the womb door:

Now that the state of becoming
  is happening to me,
I concentrate my thoughts
  without distraction,
And, striving to maintain
  the results of good karma,
Close the womb door
And without resistance I do not enter.
This is the time for pure thought and effort.
I abandon desire
  and let go of jealousy
And meditate on the guide and his consort,
The Great Mother of Space.

THIRTY-FOURTH CHAMBER

Now I am at the threshold between involution and evolution, between the high and the low. If I fall asleep here even for a single moment I will be reborn without choice. If the concentration of consciousness is focused on the beloved and the teaching, I can succeed in becoming liberated at this late date.

Now the time is here to apply the five major methods for closing the womb door. This may be my last chance. I see males and females making love, but I won't get near them. I see them in their absolute reality as the Father-Mother, the emptiness of the shining void. I make offerings to them mentally and prostrate myself with deep devotion. I ask them for teachings, for help in obtaining a good rebirth in a school where I can practice the teachings so I can do better next time. When I take this attitude toward them, the womb door will close.

If I am about to be born male then I will feel jealousy toward the father and desire for the mother. If on the other hand I am about to be born female then I will feel envy and jealousy toward the mother and passion and desire toward the father. These passions and aggressions will cause me to be born by drawing me through the womb. I will hide between the sperm and the ovum. But I probably won't see it that way. In this stage of the labyrinth voyage my perceptions can't be trusted. So I may view myself as hiding between two trees or inside a cave.

After the fusion of the sperm and ovum I will lose consciousness until the beginning of the process of birth unless I have had special teaching about remaining fully conscious while in the womb. Otherwise I'll sleep until birth, and then as I enter the new life I will be lost on the wheel once again and tormented by needless suffering.

Once back in planetary existence I will spend the lifetime constantly dramatizing the things I was afraid of during the macrodimensional experience between lives. I'll tell stories about the bogeyman, and watch films of horrors, and read about super-beings in outer space, and wonder about extra-sensory perception and miraculous powers.

When my passions and aggressions are strong, I form my attention in this way:

> I've got such miserable karma
>   that I've wandered this far down
>   into planetary existence,
> Until here I am at the entrance to a womb!
> I'm in this situation because I've been clinging
>   to control of my destiny.
> If I go on like this trying to control
>   through passion and aggression,
> I'm going to have to wander endlessly
>   in the six lower dimensions,
> And sink beneath the sea of misery
>   for a long time.
> Therefore I resolve right now

not to feel aggression or passion again.
I will let them go forever,
  along with the desire for control.
Trying to control and have my way have
  only brought me torment and pain.
Therefore I say goodbye to them.
I will never again feel
  aggression and passion.
They are gone forever!

If I concentrate my full attention and sincerity on it, I will succeed in closing the womb door.

THIRTY-FIFTH CHAMBER

If the womb still remains open and I am about to enter, then it can still be closed by the next meditation on the illusory nature of all experience.

I concentrate my attention in this way:

No matter what I think is happening or what I think I see, I am only the Clear Shining Light. The Father-Mother, the storms, the thunder, the whirlwind, the terrifying apparitions, the guides and my fears are only the thought-forms of my consciousness folding and unfolding.

Whatever I have experienced on any realm is only the projection of my own consciousness. The only genuine experience I have ever had is that of being the Clear Luminous Void of the Void. No matter what it seems to be, that is the only reality. Only I, the Clear and Shining Void, am real.

What good is it to desire an empty and unreal illusion? What good will it do me to cling to an unreal apparition as if it were solid and could protect me? What am I afraid of? There is nothing real besides myself as the Clear Shining Light, and so there is nothing that can hurt me, because there is nothing to hurt.

I have been pretending that what is real is unreal, and that what doesn't exist does exist. Can it be that I need something to exist so desperately that I am willing to do this to myself? Since all these things are simply the images which I place on my own essential self, the void itself, there is no sense in clinging to them.

Even the essential self itself, the void of the void, is non-existent in reality, and has been nonexistent from the very beginning. Even this voice, this teaching and the necessity for it are nonexistent. There never was nor will there ever be a world, nor have there ever been or ever will be six lower dimensions of inhabitants in which to be born.

I have been walking in a dream, dreaming as if there were a dream, resisting as if there were something to resist, but now I resist no longer as there is no other: no karma, no self, no void, no wombs, no male, no female, no birth, no death, no labyrinth, no reality, no unreality. Only my own endless endlessness remaining with no beginning and no end. Now it is finished, and I am done with my desire, aggression, resistance, attractions, thoughts, experience. I am ready now to be what I am. I am that I am. There is no other.

By concentrating all my thoughts and beingness on this and allowing no other belief to enter into my consciousness, the reality of the womb and the fight to resist rebirth are destroyed. When the belief in a centralized self is destroyed there is nothing to be reborn. If I am willing to renounce all experience, not only with the thoughts and heart but also from the being, then all womb doors will certainly be closed and there will be no rebirth.

THIRTY-SIXTH CHAMBER

If after all this the womb entrance still isn't closed and the belief in experience and existence can't be dissolved because I still insist on being someone or something in particular and having something happen to me, then I will concentrate my consciousness in the following way:

All substances are my own projected forms of consciousness and this consciousness is nothing but the uncreated unborn emptiness of the unobstructed luminous light of the void, without center and without circumference; without beginning and without end.

As I concentrate on this, I'll keep my thoughts flowing naturally, as the spring flows into the river. By allowing myself to rest naturally in stillness and silence, I can be sure that the womb door to rebirth will be closed.

All phenomena is illusion.
Neither attracted nor repelled,
Not making any sudden moves,
My habits will carry me through.

THIRTY-SEVENTH CHAMBER

These are the five methods for closing the womb door. In the macrodimensions my consciousness has the ability to hear and understand anything that is said in this teaching, whether it comes from one dimension or from another. Also, all the perceptions and sensations are complete and intact even if they had been impaired during my lifetime in the human dimension. And thirdly, because when in the macrodimensions of the labyrinth I am usually overcome by fear most of the time, I therefore will be willing to listen to suggestions about getting out of that situation.

As consciousness has no roots or anchor points in the macrodimensions, it naturally is attracted to any area of attention to which it is directed, and repelled just as naturally from anything which it's told to resist. Just as a tree which on land was impossible to move even with a bulldozer, when in water can be moved with one finger, so am I in the water of the labyrinthine macrodimensions and therefore my presence is fluid and extremely easy to guide even with the smallest effort.

Therefore, it's important to direct my consciousness as a voyager on every stage of the voyage in the labyrinth—not just one or two—in order to make certain that I'll attain liberation, if not at one stage, then at another. That's the reason so many confrontations and instructions are given to me during the experience of the labyrinth and the confrontation with the Clear Light is given so many times in so many forms and variations.

THIRTY-EIGHTH CHAMBER

There are many individuals who aren't interested in liberation and meet this teaching with disinterest. They only want to create suffering around them because they are suffering through existence, and they don't know how to make the efforts necessary to liberate themselves. They may prefer to wander in the six lower dimensions rather than face the simple and terrifying reality of the pure shining Clear Light.

And so they develop minds which will keep them from confronting or even knowing about this. They keep their confusions solid by creating for themselves psychoses, insanities, drives, urges, aberrations, confusions, necessities, significances, purposes, goals, aims, needs and problems. In this way they keep themselves too busy trying to handle all of that to be able to think about or remember the situation as it really is. All the effort to become awake is simply another of those mind games designed to maintain sleep.

There isn't any effort that needs to be made in order to awaken. In fact, it's just the opposite. I'll stop making efforts to remain asleep, and simply cease to have anything to do with action and reaction. I won't try to make anything happen or not happen. I'll let go of my efforts to maintain consciousness and reality. As those drop away I will be the only thing remaining. When there's no more struggle to be something, have something or do something, I will find myself awake.

THIRTY-NINTH CHAMBER

Even those individuals grimly holding on to the game of planetary existence can still be liberated—even here—if they will only listen to the emergency method of instruction for those below any hope of liberation. I'll guide my thoughts along this path:

I take refuge in the Clear Light. I take refuge in the beloved. I take refuge in the way of the teaching. I take refuge in the company of the brotherhood of spiritual souls.

If I can only ask for help sincerely without holding back or feeling pain due to my intense pride, I can attain liberation by taking refuge in those who guide the teaching.

FORTIETH CHAMBER

Even though I've been shown all these instructions so far on how to liberate myself, I haven't yet understood, and so now the womb door hasn't been closed and I am definitely about to take rebirth.

The signs of birth are about to appear. I'll remember that each dimension is color-coded for easy reference and identification, so I should be aware of the color I am seeing as well as the form. I'll pay attention to details and I'll be able to gather all the information I need in order to choose properly. The details are more important than the gross form.

I'll see a lake with white birds on it. I won't go there. It's a place where the teaching hasn't taken root, so I should avoid it.

I'll see a huge white mansion of very high aesthetic design. If I can enter there, I should do it.

I'll see a lake with horses around it. I must not be drawn to it, because, even though I can fulfill my desires of pleasure there, it's a place for material trips only, and the teaching hasn't taken root in it yet.

I'll see a lake with cattle. Even though I could have a long and peaceful life there, the teaching hasn't taken root in it, so I should avoid it.

If I see soft white temples and highly formalized buildings on hilltops, then I am going to be born into the Sun-Absolute. I'll enter there if I can.

If I see glades with large ferns, or beautiful groves of small leafed trees and winding streams or tight small wheels of fire looking like slowly revolving pinwheels, I won't get attracted to it. I'll feel revulsion and disgust toward it.

If I see caves and holes in the ground or under hills as if through a foggy mist, I won't enter there. I may also see straw huts, wooden shacks, or abandoned railroad cars and engine barns. I won't duck in there no matter what seems to be chasing me.

If I see tree stumps, charred black shapes sticking up from the ground, shallow caves and patches of burnt ground, then I am about to be born as a hungry ghost. I'll think of unbearable hunger and thirst, and I'll be able to resist it. I'll get a feeling of intense disgust toward that landscape. I won't under any circumstances think of it as a place in which to hide. And I won't run into any large black monoliths. If I fall asleep now it will all be over in an instant.

If I hear songs being sung about battle, or see large bands of hunters or military troops marching across a desolate and dark twisted country with houses of red and black, and there are black pits alongside the black road, rocky crags and slag heaps everywhere, and a black smoky cloud over everything, I'm about to be born into the hell-dimension.

If I go there I will be enslaved and made to work at destruction of the land and subjugation of the inhabitants. There are tortures and inquisition, war and continual treachery. Machinery and engines producing foul gases are everywhere, and even if I die there they have ways to revive me and force me to survive even if I don't want to. The hell-dimension is so full of pain and horror that I might never regain my stability and equilibrium long enough to get out of it. So I won't go near it at all, even in fascination that such a thing could exist. It's better to go anywhere rather than into the hell-dimension. I'll think of revulsion to it and resist it with all the will I can muster up. My fervent and powerful intention to stay away from the hell-dimension is needed now. I won't fall asleep. I'll keep awake and resist with all my effort until the womb entrance to hell is closed.

FORTY-FIRST CHAMBER

My power to remain free of rebirth is now gone, so even if I don't wish rebirth, I have no choice any more. I am being helplessly pulled and pushed, drawn into rebirth of some kind. Behind me are the ones I am afraid of, and in front of me sadistic and degraded beings are pulling me along into rebirth. Confusion is all around me; everyone is shouting directions at me, telling me what to do, which birth to take, what's best for me now, and making me unable to orient myself and choose wisely and carefully.

I'll look for some sort of refuge from all this din and shouting. I see some buildings or rocks, or perhaps a cave. Maybe all there is to hide in is a clump of bushes. After I have hidden there I'll realize that I'm in a womb and that my perceptions deceived me. What I see in the last stage of the labyrinth voyage is NOT what I get. But now I am afraid to come back out, even though I still have a chance to escape from it, because they are waiting out there to get me.

FORTY-SECOND CHAMBER

I am afraid that if I leave my safe space I'll be tortured and ripped apart by those sadistic and degraded beings, or that the giant chicken will get me and peck my eyes out, or that they'll draw and quarter me for being who I am. However bad it may seem to take that birth, I'll do it rather than face those hordes of demons, those hounds of hell, once again.

FORTY-THIRD CHAMBER

If I want to fight off the pursuers, I should immediately and without taking refuge in a hiding place, visualize the beloved as a huge and terrible demon with large thick limbs, standing in an attitude of wrath and anger. I'll have the beloved crush all those evil forces into the ground. Then while protected from these evil beings, I'll have the opportunity to choose a womb more or less at my leisure and make the proper choice according to my needs as a voyager.

There was no need for panic after all. If a bunch of demons are after me, I'll simply remember that they are my demons, and I'll just make a bigger demon to stop them.

FORTY-FOURTH CHAMBER

All these gods and demons have taken form through the power of my beliefs about reality. At this point probably the best thing I can do is meditate on the great emptiness of the void of luminous shining Clear Light, but if I can't do that, I can at least take a bigger part in the drama that's going on by creating a bigger and better demon out of the beloved which is my own teaching essential self, formed out of my own consciousness.

If even that isn't possible for me, then I'll just withdraw from the whole drama.

FORTY-FIFTH CHAMBER

If I'm still being forced to enter a womb, then I might as well make the best of it. Since I now possess the supernatural power to know all the particulars of any single incarnation or lifetime, I have some idea of the options and choices available to me. I'll choose a lifetime as if I were buying a used car. There are higher births in the upper realms and lower births in the three lower dimensions. I might even be able to obtain a rebirth in the realm of pure light.

To transfer to a pure realm of higher being, into the realm of Clear Shining Light, I'll concentrate my attention in this way:

Alas, what a bummer that after all this time floundering around in the stinking swamp of planetary existence, after countless ages of creation and destruction, without beginning and without end, while so many others were able to liberate themselves, I haven't been able to liberate myself or even ask for help.

Now I'm going to get on with it, even here in the place of rebirth. It's not too late even now. From this moment on I feel sickened by the six lower dimensions. There's nothing there for me. I don't want any part of them. There's nothing to learn there, nowhere to hide, nothing but suffering and filth. I'm tired of them. Now it's time for me to give up living in the six lower dimensions, so I'm going to bring about my spontaneous rebirth in a lotus flower at the feet of the beloved in the pure realm of the Clear Shining Light. I'm going to bathe in the pure light and wash off all this foul reeking crap that's been accumulating on me. I feel filthy and disgusted by all worldly accumulations. I have to be cleansed of them. Now I'm going. I'm going. I'm being born in the realm of luminous Clear Light and the beloved will cleanse me. I can feel the purity. I can feel it. I can feel it. I'm going.

FORTY-SIXTH CHAMBER

This isn't working out very well for me. I'll try to hang on, third time's the charm.

If I start smelling something very sweet, really sickeningly sweet, then I'm about to be born as a horsefly in a pile of dung. Whatever it looks like, if it smells sweet or looks foggy or cloudy, I won't get near it. I'll back off, using the power of revulsion and disgust, and choose another womb entrance instead.

I'll focus my attention in the following way to guide my thoughts:

I will be born as a being in the line of the teaching, within the school of the teaching, and work in the teaching for the good of all sentient beings everywhere. I will take birth with a father and mother who are embodiments of the labyrinth guide, and who are within the realm of the practice of the teaching. I will take a biological machine with merits and grace which can be used for the benefit of all sentient beings. I will practice the teaching in my new birth and during that lifetime I will perfect myself toward liberation so that all beings everywhere might benefit from my liberation in the next labyrinth voyage. I will not die again unprepared for liberation.

I'll concentrate fully on this intention, which will open a suitable womb. Immediately upon entering such a special womb I should sanctify it and treat it as a temple dedicated to the beloved who is myself as the Clear Light. I'll ask the beloved to transmit the teaching to me during that lifetime. It's within my power and right to direct the actions of the beloved in bringing about my liberation. That's what the beloved is there for. But I have to ask for it before it will come about. I will be sure to ask.

If I can't ask the beloved for help, then that's called pride and arrogance of ego. If I can't ask, then I'll just have to suffer some more until I can. And the moment that I do ask to bring about my liberation, the beloved will do it. That's because the beloved is the component of my consciousness that has the single job of liberating me. That's its only function. But there is a safety factor to insure that I won't be automatically liberated until I'm ready for it—I have to consciously and deliberately ask for my liberation and then trust the beloved to bring about the conditions of my liberation. Then I'll just take my liberation. That's all there is to it.

All I have to do is get rid of my distrust, sleep, unconscious actions, ego struggle, desires, attachments, passions and aggressions. Then I'll throw away my pride and arrogance and ask for help. It's no good to ask for help when I'm down. It's when I'm god that I ask for help in my liberation. That's when it will do some real good.

FORTY-SEVENTH CHAMBER

It's possible that a womb might appear good or bad, or I might have feelings of like or dislike about one womb or another. Again, I can't trust my impressions in this stage of the labyrinth voyage, and so the great secret here is to remain perfectly neutral and impartial, in a state of high indifference about rebirth. In this state of high indifference there is no good, no bad, no desire, no resistance, no approval, no disapproval, no passion, no disgust, no apathy, no aggression. I will just stay pure.

FORTY-EIGHTH CHAMBER

If I can't let go of all that, and I am still having trouble choosing a lifetime, no matter what happens from now on I'll concentrate on my teacher, or if possible, on the beloved in the Clear Light and hold fast on that visualization. I'll call my teacher by name. I'll give up my attachments to my old reality now. I'll give up my friends, my relations, my knowledge, my understanding of how it used to be, my influence and my power. I'll give up my material accumulations; I will get more in this next lifetime. I hate to start accumulating all over again, and it's going to be tough to break in a new biological machine to my old karmic habits, but I'm going to have to let go of my desire to have my former lifetime and biological machine back.

FORTY-NINTH CHAMBER

I'll enter now into the soft blue light of the human dimension or the soft white light of the Sun-Absolute. If I can, I'll enter the Jeweled Temples and Gardens of Delight.

The *Confrontations* while experiencing reality in the voyage through the labyrinth called the "teaching-which-liberates-by-sound" is now completed.

To those who have meditated often during their lifetime, the misleading illusions that occur at the moment of death and afterward are soon overcome, and the truth dawns on them as soon as the moment of separation of the biological machine and the common-presence-consciousness occurs.

The acquisition of experience of the labyrinth while living in a biological machine is important and can't be stressed enough; those who have recognized the real nature of their own beingness and have had some experience with the genuine identity and nature of self obtain great power during the moments of death, when the Clear Light dawns on them, and they welcome the Clear Light as a friend with whom they are very familiar, and thus merge easily with it.

Again, the meditation on the mystic path, both in the visualizing and perfecting stages, while living, will be of great benefit and influence when encountering the guides in the labyrinth. So training is of particular importance while living in a biological machine—one should hold to it; read it; commit it to memory; bear it in mind properly; read it regularly; allow the meanings of the words to form in you the understanding and sense of the method; it should be as though the words and meanings will not be forgotten even though a hundred executioners were pursuing you in a hot race.

It is called the great liberation by hearing, because even those who have committed the five boundless sins, the sins of patricide, matricide, setting two religious bodies at war, killing a saint and causing blood to flow from the body of a completed man, are sure to be liberated if they hear it by the path of the ear.

Therefore, *read it in the midst of vast congregations. Read it to heal the sick. Read it to instruct the elderly. Read it for the dead or dying even though they don't know it is being read for them—your invocations and readings are helping them to attain liberation.*

E.J. GOLD, *FIGURE AT WINDOW*, CHARCOAL ON ARCHES PAPER, 1987.

AFTERWORD

Thus priests of the labyrinth can effect the liberation of consciousness before death, during the ultimate labyrinth voyage and even into the state of rebirth. Even the lowest of the low can be turned back from the lower realms by the concentrations and invocations at the end, and can attain liberation, or at least a fortunate rebirth, simply by giving up pride and arrogance and asking for help. Thus in rebirth it is possible to meet the guide and to receive guidance and thus be liberated in that lifetime.

So it is possible for even the most unconscious individual to be helped into a lifetime which provides the opportunity to receive the teaching even if one doesn't hear the teaching until just before entrance into a womb.

This teaching is so profound that it can lead even the most evil and degraded being onto the secret path. Practice during the lifetime of letting go of attachments, passions and aggressions while under stress and extreme pressure will be better than meditations in a serene outer world environment, because only if one is able to remain serene in his being while being lashed with rawhide whips and devoured by dogs while hearing hard rock music at three thousand decibels will this instruction certainly bring about liberation at the moment before death. One must remember this teaching even if he forgets his own grandmother. There is no other teaching. This is it.

Don't forget that liberation is not necessarily awakening, but part of the experience of the experiencer. It feels better than hanging out in the six lower dimensions, and enhances awakening by making it more possible. But after awakening you won't mind being anywhere or nowhere.

Liberation makes the dream a whole lot better, and gives relief from suffering. But real awakening is simply waking up from the dream and letting the dream go on with you or without you. When you no longer want to manipulate the dream and make it better, you'll be willing to wake up. And when you wake up, you wake up.

This book should be proclaimed in the ears of all living persons everywhere; it should be read over the pillows of all persons who are ill, troubled, anxious or wishing instruction in the art of dying; it should be read at the site of all corpses; it should be broadcast over the media of all nations.

This book is the description of the method of expanding lives to reach out over many biological machines, times, conditions, deaths and dimensions. It is the method of the Bodhisattvas, the Siddhis and the Buddhas.

Liberation will be won simply by not disbelieving it when hearing it; giving it the benefit of the doubt is enough to be able to begin to hear this doctrine and use it to attain your liberation.

Disseminate this book. Through having heard it only once, even though one has no comprehension of what the subject matter is, or what the meaning of the reading is, it will be remembered in the voyage through the labyrinth without a word being omitted, for the intellect becomes ninefold more lucid in the clear state of the voyager in the labyrinth.

May this book of my wiseacrings be of real benefit to all sentient beings everywhere, and may it bring about the real liberation and real awakening of all. Good luck, and hang loose.

APPENDIX A

TABLE OF CORRESPONDENCES COLOR CODING OF THE SIX DIMENSIONS

Sun-Absolute:
    Color: Soft white
Basic element: Space
Radiation: Blue

Hell Dimension:
    Color: Smoky gray
Basic element: Form
Radiation: White

Human Dimension:
    Color: Soft blue
Basic element: Sensation
Radiation: Yellow

Ghost Dimension:
    Color: Soft pale yellow
Basic element: Perception
Radiation: Red

Purgatory-Dimension:
    Color: Soft deep red
Basic element: Concept
Radiation: Green

Brute Dimension:
    Color: Soft pale green
Basic element: Consciousness
Radiation: Rainbow or prismatic image

TENDENCIES ERASED BY THE RAYS COMING FROM THE CONSCIOUSNESS COMPONENTS

Blue: Karmic attachments and tendencies
White: Violent aggression—antagonism, anger, hatred
Yellow: Pride, arrogance, inability to wonder
Red: Intense desire, passions, uncontrollable hungers
Green: Envy, jealousy, rivalry, competitiveness
Rainbow: Unconsciousness, apathy, sleep

It can be said that the cause of all the problems in the labyrinth is trying to hold on to form. In the first stage, one tries to hold on to the form which the components of consciousness had before breaking up into basics.

In the second stage, one tries to hold on to the basic elemental non-structure. One tries to keep the components of consciousness in their pure basic form, incorruptible and unchangeable, so that one can eventually understand them. In the second stage one gets into the trap of studying or trying to understand the components of consciousness one at a time.

In the third stage, one tries to prevent the component parts of consciousness from re-forming into a new consciousness formation, called "rebirth." The new form of consciousness when first built is free from interaction, and therefore is called the "womb."

After a while the five pure components of consciousness begin to interact with each other. At a point of critical mass, this becomes "birth," at Samsara, and further interactions cause the growth of apparent ego, personality and a world of experience. After fully passing through each other, they again separate until a full point of separation is reached, at Nirvana. After the mid-point of separation they again come together, and passing through each other create a reality, mind, ego and experience through the merging of their light into a rainbow of complexity.

APPENDIX B

LABYRINTH GAMES

1. **Form Change** games: green slime, snake games, worm games, becoming waves, growing fur, form melting, becoming planets, blobs, stretching arms, becoming puddles.
2. **Adding and Subtracting Heads, Arms, Legs, Fingers** game.
3. **Cheshire Cat** game: dropping off the form until only the smile is left.
4. **Slinky** game: boing-boing spring.
5. **Becoming Star Bodies** game: star-filled bodies.
6. **Becoming Very Old** game: wrinkles, brown, gray, crumbling to dust.
7. **Becoming Very Ugly** game: see who can be the ugliest.
8. **Snap** game: snapping people into different spaces.
9. **Upscaling/Downscaling** games: follow the leader.
10. **Gross-out** games: room gets filled with rising shit, cannibalism, disease games—diseases are transmitted, body rot game.
11. **Sliding Down Razor Blade** game.
12. **Stubborness** games: (last one to stop being a rock).
13. **Revenge** games: throw someone into dream world making them work thousands of lifetimes to climb back up, then throw them down again just as they upscale.
14. **Disappearing** games: hide and seek.
15. **Seance** games: bringing famous people forms into the room.
16. **T.V.** games: put the group entertainer "in the screen" and make him perform.
17. **Weather** games: temperature changes, rain from ceiling, coldness.
18. **Balling** games: everyone becomes a crystal ball filled with stars.
19. **Tilting Room** game: also, shrinking room, up-side-down room, no air in room, disappearing into the walls.
20. **Muffing** game: walls are encrusted with crud.

21. **Reminiscence** game: everyone takes on different masks.
22. **Everybody Becomes the Same** game: everyone becomes the same form or personality, then try to form relationships.
23. **Holocaust** games: roomspace blows up in everyone's face.
24. **Great Drama** games: re-enacting great dramas.
25. **Pain and Torture** games.
26. **Violence** games.
27. **Embarrassing Moments** games: re-enacting most embarrassing moments in various dream lives
28. **I Don't Know** game: everyone forgets truth, then seeks someone who knows.
29. **All Alone** games: continual dwelling on being all-one, alone.
30. **I Know Something You Don't Know** game.
31. **Jealousy** games: musical chairs relationships.
32. **Games of Scale:** from atom to universe and back again.
33. **Bouncing Around Walls** game.
34. **Making One Wall of Room into a Window, Scary Forms Appear at Window** game.
35. **Deformities** game: lumpy funny bodies.
36. **Harmony** games: being chords, pure notes.
37. **Beautiful Light Pattern** games: being most beautiful, powerful, etc., light pattern.
38. **Aesthetic** games: making most beautiful things.
39. **Perfection** games: being most perfect for longest time.
40. **Being Food** games: last to get eaten wins; who is being the Thanksgiving turkey?
41. **Explanation** games.
42. **Finding New Unexplored Space** game.
43. **Psychology** games: complex, simple, etc.
44. **Being Afraid** games.
45. **Discovering New Life Forms** games.
46. **Upside-down Room** game.
47. **Being Tired of Games** game.
48. **Crack in the Cosmic Egg** game: room begins to split apart.
49. **Machine** games: becoming parts of machines, computers, computer in chest.

50. **Shatter** games: explosion games.
51. **Speeding up/Slowing down** games.
52. **Entrapment** games: spider web spaces.
53. **Perpetual Entertainment Machine** game:
    TV screen on one wall and you snap someone
    into it, forcing them to tap dance forever.
54. **Let's Let One Thing From Out There
    Into Here** game.
55. **Tweak the Room Slightly Out of Alignment** game.
56. **Beauty and the Beast** games: the most beautiful colors,
    sounds, creations, textures, etc. and then the most ugly, dis-
    gusting, horrid colors, sounds, creations, etc.
57. **Mischief** games: froggy, hit someone as though the one next
    to them did it, etc.
58. **Strip Poker** game: dismantling limbs instead of clothes, and
    then pretending you forgot how to do it.
59. **Dread** games: any moment now the worst possible thing is
    about to happen—many variations on this theme.
60. **Alien Planet/Galaxy Contact** games: pretending you don't
    know anything about TX-17; making incredible efforts to
    contact them. And when you do you have the tremendous task
    of deciphering their language, understanding their history,
    etc.

There's lots of pretend games where you agree to blot out
your knowledge/experience about a certain period in Earth
history or pretend not to remember anything about being
exiled to Selusa Secundus, etc. and it becomes very impor-
tant/urgent to explore that. But there's always some asshole in
the room who, right when the game is culminating and all the
eons of exploration and work are about to pay off, rolls all
over the floor yuk-yukking, slapping his thigh and blowing
the whole number.

That is also another version of the No Satisfaction, No
Rewards game, which usually leads into the Crucifixion
games, which usually lead into the Great Religions of the
Universe games which lead into the Great Saints, Martyrs,
etc. games, which lead into the Sodom and Gomorrah games

which lead into the Puritan-Persecution games which lead into the Barf games (just to break the pattern) which lead into the Science and Scientists games, which lead into the Great Political and Historical Figures (and their defamation) games, at which point, the same asshole who won't let anyone else play their games wants to play WAR.

At this point, he gets sent plummeting back, screaming and cursing, to the accompanying jeers and cheers of his fellow roommates, to the trilobite stage. All the rest rock-out and wait for his return. Just as he sets his fingers on the edge of the floor and is about to haul himself back into his homeroom after eons of agonizing evolution, they freak him out so badly that he plummets back to the algae stage. And so on, ad infinitum.

61. **Kings and Queens at Court** games: ritualistic games with strange twists and innovative patterns and customs.
62. **Medieval Torture** games: guillotine, rack, cat o' nine tails.
63. **Tag** games and variations upon.
64. **Competitions**: the most ugly, beautiful, fastest, slowest, strangest, grotesque, ethereal (most anything—or nothing).
65. **Skull-out, Puddle-out, Slime-out** games.
66. **Enchantment** games: a version of **Snap** where you use music, images, etc., to try to mesmerize the others.
67. **Power** games: you're in my power/I'm in your power.
68. **Home Movies** game: what I did during my summer vacation.
69. **Nostalgia** games: those were the good old days— remember when . . .
70. **Gods and Goddesses** games: Zap! I'm Zeus! Poof! I'm Apollo!
71. **Artisans** games: look what I just made!
72. **Evolve/Devolve** games: tail-brain duty in a brontosaurus.
73. **Sports** games: people become a ball, hoop, puck, etc.
74. **Take-it Way-out** games: essentially how close to the "edge" can you go? See how long you can hang out with "uh-oh sensations."
75. **High-sensation** games.

APPENDIX C

REBIRTH STATIONS

The following list of rebirth stations is only partial. A detailed and comprehensive list can be found in the Practitioner's Edition of the *American Book of the Dead*.

The Barracks: thousands of barrack buildings set up along street lines. Men, women and children all occupy these as if a city.

Rare Book Shop: leather covered books everywhere. Shop is deep and narrow, shelves on either side as one enters. Aisle goes back to rear of store. Elderly woman is shopkeeper.

Mountain Cabin and Car Crash Incident: party, rows of cars parked below house, hear cars crash, see toy cars from above, river of blood flows down mountain road.

2001-type Morgue: bodies laid out on tables, one sits up, talks to another on right.

Concrete Underground Garage: after holocaust, bandaged victims lie on floor in corner.

Long Beach Strand after Eco-disaster: people on beach starving, hustling trying to get boats to get off beach, etc.

Island: tidal wave hits, women and men put children in boats to save them from drowning. Beach scene, shows only tiny portion of island left; people miles out are only waist-deep in water. Wailing and crying of grownups. Some adults take children out of boats and climb in them.

Underwater City: iron sphere to reach surface after earthquake destroys city under sea.

Red Dirt Road: construction and road grading in mountains on lonely road at night. Dog pack is close, and dangerous.

Bungalow Village: theater nearby. Cement walkways between are narrow. Night scene. Millions of bungalows as far as the eye can see, except for theater, no other buildings in sight.

Grand Central Station: giant hallway leading to central room. Floating halfway between ceiling and floor, each millions of miles away. In central room are giant slugs crawling on the walls. There are doors in the hallways. Other groups are seen emerging from their rooms, or floating toward or away from the central room. Guides float past, offering help to any who require Travelers' Aid.

Telepathic Serpents: the snake people. Standing in room with soft walls and an orange light. High ceiling.

The Empty City: low buildings, cold, bitter wind. Nobody on streets. No lights in windows.

Endless Apartment Projects: apartment buildings are in decay, ruin. People live in them, scrounge for food, etc.

Room with Visitor: someone opens door periodically and looks in to see if occupant is alert. If not, something dreadful will happen.

Standing Forever: swaying back and forth, the individual in this room can never sit, lie down or lean against anything.

Plastic Covered Theater Seats: become organs in giant body.

Parquet Floor Room: looking down, can't help levitating up and out of room, seemingly going upward forever. Woman below reaches for legs to pull down, but can't reach them. She is crying and wailing for upward flier to come back.

Doll House: big eye looks through window at people inside house.

Monkey Man in Trailer: hands over head, crouching on bunk in back. Computer readout is on right side. Is manlike, gray haired, no body hair, just gorilla-like with long arms, short legs, hangs from upper bunk railing.

Fun House: old fashioned type funhouse, walkthrough not ride.

Riverworld: canal houses on canal streets. Corner building has secret room in back, in which sanctuary is available.

Interstellar Copper Disk Radio: resonator, lines of force as sephiroth. Image of star being appears in center at tiphareth. Image similar to "demon" of superstition.

Stuck in the Wall: "chalkline walls," walk through, lose it, stuck in wall, relax, work way back out again.

Tribunal Council: exile to earth, must leave body in care of authorities, take human biological machine while on earth, perform task (mission) and then allowed to come back and resume life in real (beautiful) body. This as punishment for imaginary crime for which everyone facing tribunal is framed so they will accept missions on earth. Recruiting method, not actual punishment.

Cave of Ancients: caves occupied by eternal beings, who can never leave their individual cells. They send messengers back and forth between them. Linked telepathically, they also have vision of entire structure of caves as a single entity.

Primordial Being: flip-flop jellyfish-like creature suspended in space, continually and compulsively changing form every moment (or every eternity). Occupied by cells within, conforming to Cave of Ancients, silent screaming. Continual change is torture to this being, who wants help of occupants of each cell.

Broadway Scene: stone buildings on wide street. Similar to old New York Broadway uptown. Early morning, there are streetcar tracks in street, island divider in center of street.

House of Many Mansions: hallways of powder blue with French doors and French trim around them. Each door opens to tiny room, containing desk, three antique chairs, orange antique desk light.

Crystal Ball and Breathing Stone: man sits in chair, arms and legs retracting. He is becoming spherical.

Grand Hotel: turn of the century Victorian hotel, large corridors, cage elevators, grand ballroom, couples dance, but no band on bandstand.

Balcony around Black Hole: into which people are falling toward rebirth. Shaped like horserace track or running track. No bars at edge, easy to get pushed over by enormous crowd behind as they move closer to center of auditorium-sized room.

Coliseum Upstairs: gym downstairs, sub-basement pool indoors. On hilltop, out of populated area. Winding road leading up to it.

Bijou Theater: rats, musty, plain white light on screen, audience reacting with tears, laughter, etc., projecting their own images onto the screen. Upstairs bathrooms, mixed sexes, liquid all over floor, open commodes and hundreds of urinals.

Marble Bathroom: giant public restroom all in marble, columns, patterned floor, etc. Janitor, ultra high ceiling, row of urinals on left, sinks in center, toilets on right.

Office Building: with penthouse on top (4th) floor. Open within, courtyard in center of building. Decor similar to mid 1940s style.

Apartment: stage apartment has parquet floors, orange light, etc., with theater seats above similar to operating theater.

Roundhouse Car Barn: place where railroad engines were once stored, now empty, with tracks running in, meeting at center. Dark office doors, glassed, on right and left, with narrow hallways running off to right and left between offices. Looks like 1940s warehouse with railroad tracks.

Barnyard with a Bull and a Giant Chicken: barn on right, another, two-story, barn on left. Doors to barn on right on ground floor. Door to barn on left on second floor, can only be reached by outside stairs going up side of building.

Recruiting Center: like loading docks. Behind this is barracks, behind barracks is hospital, jail, etc.

Prison Farm: entrance is farmlike, leads to small barracks. Surrounding whole place is electrified barbed wire fence above chain link fencing. Park-like path leads through. Small hills above lead in and down to the left to the farm.

Hill Village: freeway interchange leads to over-the-hill mountain road, down into a ravine in which is a tiny village, mostly children. People are artisans and craftsmen. Other road leads up to hill house.

Hillside House: on hillside, grass grows around it, multi-level in half-story increments. Enter house from left side into the kitchen. To right is studio type living room, another room or rooms below this.

Farmhouse: as one comes in, farmhouse single story New England type is on left, out-building on right. Chickens in yard.

Library: machine in library waiting room and pickup order desk (on right of desk) has "sanity certificates" for citizens, fifty cents. Very high ceilings. Wait for number to be called on light board.

ABOUT THIS BOOK

This new edition enhances the impact of this striking and exciting book. Here in short form is the substance of basic human esoteric teachings given in modern language.

What is more important in one's here-and-now belief systems (simulations of Reality) than those clustering around one's birth, death, and apparent re-birth? Can we escape this repetitive round of incarnation-carnation-excarnation? Is there a someone who can be free of this repeating tape-loop of existences, of repeated human-non-human states of being? If there is, that someone may need help to get off the round, the eternal dance in a circular path, and enter other domains beyond it. This book is one set of understandable injunctions on how to escape, or how to choose a more satisfying labyrinthine voyage on the next choice-point: at death, at rebirth, during Transit. Stimulated by this book plus the *Simulations of God*, I wrote and narrated an ECCO training film: *Simulations of God*. (In reality, of course, ECCO wrote it with me as their agent).

What is ECCO? In order to give one an understanding, I quote from chapter Zero of *Dyadic Cyclone* (written with my lady Antonietta).

"Several years ago, I enunciated a format (a principle) for such a concatenation of events, somewhat as follows:

There exists a *Cosmic Coincidence Control Center* (CCCC), with a galactic substation called Galactic Coincidence Control (GCC). Within GCC is a Solar System Control Unit (SSCU), within which is the Earth Coincidence Control Office ECCO (sometimes mistakenly shortened to ECO, as in ECOSYSTEMS and in ECOLOGY—the study of Earth Coincidence Control Office). Down through the hierarchy of coincidence control (from cosmic to galactic to solar system to Earth) is a chain of command with greater and greater specification of regulation of coincidences appropriate to each level in the system. The assignments of responsibilities from the top to the bottom of this system of control is by a set of regulations, which translated by ECCO for us human beings is somewhat as follows:

"To all humans:

If you wish to control coincidence in your own life on the planet Earth, we will cooperate and determine those coincidences for you under the following conditions:

(1) You must know/assume/simulate our existence in ECCO.

(2) You must be willing to accept our responsibility for control of your coincidences.

(3) You must exert your *best capabilities* for your survival programs and your own development as an advancing/advanced member of ECCO's earthside corps of controlled coincidence workers. You are expected to use your best intelligence in this service.

(4) You are expected to expect the unexpected every minute of every hour of every day and of every night.

(5) You must be able to remain conscious/thinking/reasoning no matter what events we arrange to happen to you. Some of these events will seem cataclysmic/catastrophic/overwhelming: remember, *stay aware, no matter what happens/apparently-happens to you.*

(6) You are in our training program for life: there is no escape from it: we (not you) control the long term coincidences. You (not we) control the shorter term coincidences by your own efforts.

(7) Your major mission on Earth is to discover/create that which we do control: the long term coincidence patterns; you are being trained on Earth to do this job.

(8) When your mission on planet Earth is completed, you will no longer be required to remain/return there.

(9) Remember the motto passed to us (from GCC via SSCU): *'Cosmic Love is absolutely ruthless and highly indifferent: it teaches its lessons whether you like/dislike them or not.'* "

(End of Instructions)

This book can be seductive. ECCO (through Gold) set up a beautiful trap for you. After you read it, ask yourself, "What is the trap?"

If you can correctly answer that question, you are free.

John C. Lilly, M.D.

Labyrinth Readers Course

It is our experience that anyone with a sincere interest is able to develop the skills and learn the art of being a labyrinth reader by completing the Labyrinth Readers Course. We offer the course in three ways:

1. The Online Labyrinth Readers Course

This course meets weekly online in a chat room and the instructor helps the participants develop the necessary skills. The text used is *The American Book of the Dead* by E.J. Gold. This 15-week course teaches competency in working with the sick and dying to assist them with passage by maintaining a close, strong contact with them throughout the complete reading cycle. The cyberspace environment enhances the dynamic nature of this course.

2. Workshops

We offer workshops to develop the practical skills needed to use *The American Book of the Dead*. Learn how to involve yourself as a guide with others in your daily life, and develop lifelong practices which will strengthen your ability to be attentive and present during your own passage. We can come to your site or you can attend the workshops held in California several times each year. A one-evening to a three-day workshop can be arranged.

3. Correspondence Course

This is the classic Bardo instruction manual with exercises and practices to develop the skills of a guide. The mail order course requires 10 weeks for completion under the guidance of our experienced practitioners. The course comes complete with workbook, question and answer material, and can be used by an individual working alone or with a group.

Private edition publication, spiralbound,
with answer booklet and reading log booklet.

For more information or for an upcoming schedule of courses and fees contact:

LABYRINTH READERS SOCIETY

P.O. Box 370, Nevada City, CA 95959.
(800) 869-0658 or (530) 477-8101 or fax: (530) 272-0184
online:lrs@slimeworld.org or patelrs@slimeworld.org
or http://www.slimeworld.org/lrs
website:http://www.slimeworld.org/lrs

LABYRINTH READERS SOCIETY

The Labyrinth Readers Society, a division of a non-profit organization, has been working to provide trainings in the arena of death and dying for over 30 years. Its mission is to nurture a heightened awareness of how to assist one another through final passage, and in doing so, deepen the understanding of life. Utilizing versions of *The American Book of the Dead* by E.J. Gold, members of the Labyrinth Readers Society provide the service of reading for the sick and dying as well as training others to do so in times of illness, crisis or bereavement.

Dying is a natural part of living. Dying is the personal experience of the Being letting go of its physical form. Helping someone relax into a peaceful, attentive passage calls for a dedicated guide: one who cares enough to assist another through this transition. To read *The American Book of the Dead* aloud for the benefit of another helps that Being remain focused, not distracted while going through the Bardos.

If You Are a Labyrinth Reader, This is What You'll Do:

Stay present. Be there with the individual; be open, simple and in the present. Listen with your heart, not your mind. There's often anger, denial and fear before acceptance of the inevitable.

Be responsive without trying to fix the pain. The key to dying is allowing oneself to relax. Embracing natural fears of the unknown with acceptance and joy brings one through difficult moments, expanding the capacity to surrender and let go.

Be attentive. Attention is designed to carry us through the transitions of death and birth. The state between death and birth, for which our western culture has no words, becomes visible to the terminal patient as passage approaches.

Be sincere and constant. Being honest and speaking directly helps the individual maintain a connection with his/her own purity and strength.

Be a terminal midwife. The experience between death and birth carries with it disorientation and forgetfulness. Being there as a midwife is an act of compassion, assisting the individual in remaining as conscious as possible through transition.

Read aloud. The 49 days of readings from the *American Book of the Dead* are extremely useful instructions for those traveling in the Bardos.

Books, Recordings, Videos Available from Gateways

If you like what you see in this book, please take note of the following additional texts, videos and CDs.

The Great Adventure
by E.J. Gold. ISBN: 0-89556-110-7, BK081, $15.95.
Deepening the understanding of a compassionate, non-sentimental approach to the great voyage that every human will undertake, this book is recommended for every reader of spiritual literature.

Book of Sacraments
by E.J. Gold. ISBN: 0-89556-072-0, BK078, $12.95.
A book of readings and illustrations that has a universal, nondenominational appeal.

Angels Healing Journey
by E.J. Gold. ISBN: 0-89556-111-5, BK079, $15.95.
This is a practical and beautiful book of angelic prayers for help, for healing and for guiding loved ones after their final passage, appealing to those who feel a close connection with the world of angels.

Handbook for the Recently Deceased
by Dr. Claude Needham. ISBN: 0-89556-068-2, BK074, $16.95.
Fortunately for you, this book has been written with you in mind. But be warned—this book contains great and amazing secrets meant only for the eyes of the dead. So, if you are not dead, whatever you do, don't order this book!

Using the ABD for Healing
a talk by E.J. Gold. CDT208, $12.97

The Making of the ABD
E.J. Gold. 2 CD set, CDT039, $22.97

Making of the ABD
Part 2-interview with E.J. Gold. CDT267, $12.97

Sacred Prayers-Readings from ABD
by E.J. Gold. CDM200, $49.00

Lazy Man's Guide-Reading
by E.J. Gold with music. 4 CD Set, CDM125 , $49.97

Journey Through the Great Mother
a guided induction with music
CDM017, $16.97

Bardo Reaction Video Test
computer visual experience that exposes "bardo hooks," VID044,
$19.95

Darkside Dreamwalker
E.J. Gold, beginning induction video for lucid dreaming. VID 118,
$19.95

Past Lives Healing Journey
E.J. Gold, a past-lives karma cleanser. VID 120,$19.95

Angels Healing Journey
E.J. Gold, a cybernetic vision quest. VID 119, $19.95

Practical Guide to
the Labyrinth - The Series

A brilliant and colorful photographic journey through Bardo Town™, the HO scale model tabletop layout built by E.J. Gold and his team of psychic scientists during the years 1992-1997, and photographed by him at that time. Bardo Town™ is the result of over three decades of planning, measuring 75' x 54' when finished.

Hundreds of photographs capturing Bardo Town™ in living color are available on CD-ROM, including behind-the-scenes photos that illustrate the effort that went into the production of this enormous scale model, complete with sound bytes to enhance the experience.

Practical Guide to the Labyrinth - Part 1 is available on the following website:

www.gatewaysbooksandtapes.com

Additional websites of interest for Bardo-Training events:

www.urthgame.com
www.theclearlight.com
www.thecaregiverwebsite.com
www.idhhb.com

LIST OF ILLUSTRATIONS
BY E. J. GOLD

Dear Reader of the *American Book of the Dead*:

Having completed this book, you may feel the wish to be of service for the benefit of all Beings everywhere by applying the Teaching contained in the *American Book of the Dead*. If you wish to pursue this path further, a professional *Labyrinth Readers Course* is offered on-line, by correspondence, and in person—your location or ours. We will work with you and/or your group to help you use this material.

The *Labyrinth Readers Course* teaches you to be competent in working with those who are dying, to prepare them for Expulsion and to maintain a close, strong contact with them throughout the complete reading cycle. The LRS maintains a reading service for all those who want this help. You can become eligible to join the circle of those reading for others as they travel through the Bardo.

Gateways also distributes *Angels Healing Journey* and *The Book of Sacraments* as excellent companions to the *American Book of the Dead*. You will find these books in your local bookstore—or you can contact Gateways Books & Tapes to order direct or to request the latest catalog. You may want to visit the Labyrinth Readers Society website at slime-world.org/lrs and find out about joining our current activities.

Write:
Gateways Books & Tapes
P.O. Box 370-A
Nevada City, CA 95959-0370

Phone:
(800) 869-0658 *(in the USA)*
(530) 271-2239
(530) 687-0317 *(efax only)*

Websites:
www.gatewaysbooksandtapes.com
www.theclearlight.com

email:
info@gatewaysbooksandtapes.com or
lrs@gatewaysbooksandtapes.com

facebook:
www.facebook.com/Americanbookofthedead
www.facebook.com/groups/LRSForum